Günter Hugo Magnus

Graphic Techniques

For Designers and Illustrators

Graphic Techniques

For Designers and Illustrators

Günter Hugo Magnus

BARRON'S

Woodbury, New York • Toron

First U.S. and Canadian edition, published in 1986
by Barron's Educational Series, Inc.

© 1980 DuMont Buchverlag, Köln.

All rights for all countries with (owned by)
DuMont Book Publishing Inc. (Society with Ltd. Liability) & Co.

Limited Partnership, Cologne
Federal Republic of Germany

The title of the German original edition reads:
DuMont's Handbook for Graphic Designers
by Günter Hugo Magnus

All inquiries should be addressed to:
Barron's Educational Series, Inc.
113 Crossways Park Drive
Woodbury, New York 11797

International Standard Book No. 0-8120-5466-0

Library of Congress Catalog Card No. 86-3449

Library of Congress Cataloging-in-Publication Data

Magnus, Günter Hugo.
   Graphic techniques for designers and illustrators.

   Translation of: DuMont's Handbuch für Grafiker.
   Includes index.
   1. Commercial art—Technique.   2. Graphic arts—
Technique.   I. Title.
NC1000.M3413   1986   741.6   86-3449
ISBN 0-8120-5466-0

PRINTED IN JAPAN

6 7 8 9   9 8 7 6 5 4 3 2 1

Acknowledgments

I would like to express my special gratitude to my design students in Darmstadt and at Ohio State University, Columbus, who, as the authors of most of the work shown here and of many works not shown, made it possible for me to write this book. Many former students and friends have been generous enough to let me reprint their past and present work, and have also helped by contributing their ideas and procedures. The Mayer-Norten Group, an artists' agency, made a large number of professional illustrations available to me, and I am particularly grateful to Mr. Michael Keller for his help. I am also grateful to Mr. Guido Mangold for the details taken from the picture "My Father with His Dog" by Alex Colville (page 129).

Products that have been discontinued and processes that have recently been introduced have obliged me to do a thorough revision of my original text and to make some additions to this new English edition. I would like to express my special thanks to Mr. Iversen of Iversen and Gulielminetti, to Mr. Moser of art material service, and to Mr. Schnabel of Agfa-Gevaert for the practical tips and advice they gave me on the problems presented by the new technology.

Permissions

The author and publisher are grateful to the following publishers for granting permission to reprint their works in this book:

Illustration on page 38 from *HIGGLETY PIGGLETY POP! Or There Must Be More To Life*, story and pictures by Maurice Sendak. Copyright © 1967 by Maurice Sendak. Reprinted by permission of Harper & Row, Publishers, Inc.

Illustration on page 56 from *THE BLUE ASPIC*, by Edward Gorey. Hawthorn Books © 1968. Reprinted by permission.

We are also grateful to the following sources for supplying photos of their products that appear in the chapter on materials: Agfa-Gevaert, Inc., Waldwick, New Jersey; the Gillette Company, Paper Mate Division, Boston, Massachusetts; M. Grumbacher, Inc., New York, New York; Koh-i-Noor Rapidograph, Inc., Bloomsbury, New Jersey; Salis International, Hollywood, Florida; Steig Products, Lakewood, New Jersey; and Union Rubber, Inc., Trenton, New Jersey.

Lastly, illustrations appearing on pages 255-257 are reprinted courtesy of Letraset, Inc., Paramus, New Jersey.

Contents

Introduction

This book is primarily concerned with the plastic, 3-dimensional and perspective representation of reality on 2-dimensional surfaces, such as paper, board, canvas, or other such materials. It touches on linear, 2-dimensional, and structural representations only where these methods constitute a preliminary stage or aid to, or necessary part of, a 3-dimensional rendering.

The examples you will find here are familiar images—in various graphic forms—from our manufactured environment. You see them every day on posters, in ads, on record covers and dust jackets, in books, magazines, and catalogs, on packages, bank notes, and postage stamps, in the movies, and on television.

Many of the examples in this book were done by beginning students, working not from nature but from photographs. This process is called *graphic translation*. It has taken a long time for photography to win recognition as a legitimate aid to the graphic artist, even though Canaletto was using the camera oscura as early as the 18th century to render his Venetian scenes in perfect perspective. Well-known 19th-century painters, such as Franz von Lenbach and Franz von Stuck, photographed clients of whom they did portraits, though they did so secretly so as not to endanger their reputations as portrait painters.

Since most art students today have not received any instruction in drawing from nature, I have them work from photographs to teach them, early in their studies and in as brief a time as possible, the various techniques of representation. They obviously do not learn how to draw this way, for learning to draw is a long, indeed often a lifelong, process. But with these techniques a beginner will soon be able to execute an idea on paper.

It is particularly important for beginners, if they are to grasp a technique effectively, to view a project in the same scale in which it was produced. In this way, they can see how delicate or rough the execution is, how wide a particular penstroke or brushstroke is, how the color is applied, and what structural characteristics a color can have. For these reasons, I have, where possible, reproduced works on their original scale; and with larger works I have preferred to print a detail rather than a radically scaled-down version of the whole.

Scaling down makes imperfections and small errors disappear, makes transitions look smoother, draws uncohesive structures together, and, in most cases, improves on the original. Techniques that remain visible in the original scale often can be seen only with difficulty or not at all in a reduction.

Since reduction tends to improve on the original, many illustrators use this effect, executing their originals on a much larger scale than that of the finished reproductions. This scaling-down process also allows them to work more quickly and with a freer hand.

Conversely, a radical enlargement of a very small original can make some lines and structures more striking. This is particularly true for drawings and watercolors. A few examples are shown in the sections on copying machines.

A word on the list of materials: This list is as comprehensive as space allows. Apart from professional studios and a few compulsive and wealthy individuals, hardly any other graphic artist will have or need all these items. In connection with some processes, I mention materials, machines, and other implements that are beyond a student's modest budget and that of many drafters as well. But I mention them anyhow because they are used constantly these days, and the reader should at least be aware of them.

One rarely needs all the equipment listed here. Many modern processes, such as ColorKey Photostats, can be purchased, or are available, through graphic printing services. Then, too, most graphic artists specialize and therefore need only a limited set of materials. Some products were originally developed for technical purposes, and anyone can adapt them to his or her own needs. I have not mentioned specific brands of products, such as felt-tipped markers, that are constantly coming on to the market in a wide range of prices.

Good tools do not come cheap, and since most of the things you buy you will only need to buy once, it makes sense to purchase a somewhat more expensive, better made product than a cheaper, crudely made mass-produced item. This holds true for paper and board as well as for drafting sets, scissors, and brushes. You do not save money in the long run, for example, by buying a cheap brush that you can use for only 2 days before you have to throw it away because the hairs are sticking out like broom straws. Similarly, if you are working with color on cheap Bristol or illustration board, even Scotch tape will tear the upper layer of paper off and make retouching with a razor blade or knife impossible. Conversely, however, an inexpensive resin-based wall paint can often do the same job as a casein or acrylic paint.

Many manufacturers and art supply stores provide extensive and informative prospects and catalogs free of charge. These publications will, of course, offer more detail than the list of materials I have included here. They contain specific information on paints, transfer lettering and screens (with such brand names as Letraset, Tac-type, Zip-a-Tone), photosensitive materials (ColorKey and Chromatec), photomaterial (Copy-proof and Copychrome from Agfa), blueprint materials (Diazo), and much more.

A tip: Many shops give discounts for large orders of the same product; the larger the order, the greater the discount. So if it is possible to order with a group, as in the case of a class, it certainly pays to take advantage of these discounts.

A note on the text: Illustrations done by students are marked with an (S). Unsigned examples are by the author, unless acknowledged in the permissions list on page 5.

Materials

This is an annotated list of materials that you will find useful. As we mentioned earlier, no artist needs all these items, but you should be familiar with them and know that they are available.

1 Drawing Materials

1.0 Wooden Pencils

Wooden pencils come in the following grades:

6B, 5B: very soft, dark pencils for sketching and shading.

4B, 3B: soft pencils for sketching.

2B, B, HB, F: moderately soft pencils for sketching and drawing.

H, 2H, 3H, 4H, 5H: hard and very hard pencils for preliminary drawings, drawings, and tracing.

6H, 7H, 8H: extremely hard pencils used in preparing mechanical artwork, for executing very exacting work, and in special fields like cartography and lithography.

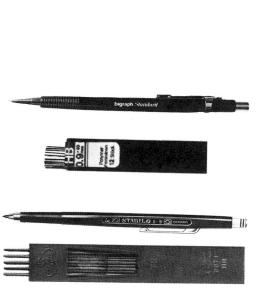

1.1 Fine-Lead Mechanical Pencils

With thin leads: .3mm, .5mm, .7mm, .9mm. These leads do not have to be sharpened; the line remains the same thickness.

Leads from 2B to 5H: There are colored leads in .5mm and .7mm.

1.2 Regular Mechanical Pencils

These are drafting pencils with normal-size leads (like those in wooden pencils) in grades 6B to 8H. They can be sharpened to a much finer point with a lead sharpener.

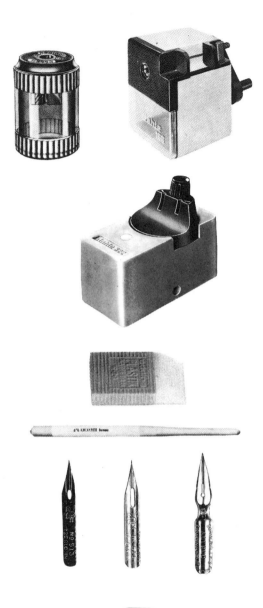

1.3 Pencil Sharpeners

Pencil sharpeners range from the simplest hand-held types to elaborate manual and electric ones.

1.4 Lead Sharpener

This is used for mechanical pencils described earlier. The major brands include Lead Pointer (Koh-I-Noor), Turquoise Lead Pointer (Eagle), Tru-Point Pencil Lead Pointer, and Dial-A-Point Lead Pointer.

1.5 Erasers

The Staedtler Mars plastic eraser and the Eberhard Faber Kneaded Rubber eraser are good erasers for both frosted acetate and paper. There are also Pink Pearl, Magic-Rub peel-off, and drafting film erasers by Koh-I-Noor.

1.6 Holder for Pen Points

These are also called penholders.

1.7 Pen Points

A wide range of points are made by the firms Hunt or Gillot for drawing in black or colored inks. Grades range from moderately soft to hard; points, from fine to extra fine.

1.8 Waterproof Drawing Ink (India Ink)

Black ink for pen and brush comes in a jar.

1.9 Black Drawing Ink

Packaged in jar, bottle, or cartridge for pen and brush, it can be thinned with distilled water.

1.10 Technical Pens

These fountain pens for special inks are used primarily for technical drawing. They come with stroke thicknesses of .13, .18, .25, .35, .5, .7, 1.0, 1.4, 2.0 mm. For most projects the stroke thicknesses .18, .25, .35, .5, and .7 are all that are needed. Major brands of technical pens are Rapidograph, Mars-700, TG, Pelikan Graphos, Faber-Castell.

1.11 Drawing Inks for Pens

Special ink for technical pens is available in black and 5 colors; it comes in cartridges and bottles.

1.12 Pen-White/Pen Opaque

This white covering ink is available in a bottle and in a bottle with a dropper for technical pens from .5mm and up and for brushes. It is useful for covering ink.

1.13 Opaque White/Graphic White

Opaque white comes in tubes and jars; mixed with water, it is used to cover ink, tempera, and gouache. It is available in a great variety of types depending on the intended use; Pelikan and Steig are among a number of manufacturers.

1.14 Liquid Paper and Thinner

This correction fluid was originally made for correcting typing errors; because of its high opacity, it can also be used for making corrections on mechanical artwork.

1.15 Drafting Set

The essential items are a compass with pencil and pen inserts, a divider, a drop compass, a centering tack (for cutting out circles).

1.16 Cutter Blade

This can be used in place of a lead in a compass to cut circles out of paper or acetate.

1.17 Cutter Compass

This compass, equipped with a steel spring, is not as likely to need adjustment after repeated cuts. For most purposes, the cutter blade mounted in a regular compass is adequate. A beam compass can also be used in a similar fashion, as can a bow compass.

1.18 Ruling Pen with Cross Joint

Use this to draw lines with a ruler in any ink or thinned paint. The cross joint facilitates cleaning. The ruling pen for curves is used for drawing curved lines with French curves in any thinned ink.

1.19 Drawing Board

Made of hard plastic laminate, wood, or formica, it comes with various edges, attachments, and surfaces. it is ideal for executing technical drawings, mechanicals, and other jobs where a large stiff steady surface is needed. It does not pay to buy a board any smaller than 12″ × 15″ (30.5 × 42 cm); a wide variety of boards and drawing tables is available.

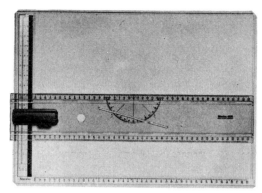

1.20 Drawing Board with Adjustable Angle

Useful for working with paints, the raised board takes on the quality of an easel and makes the work more accessible to the eye than if it were flat on a table. It is ideal for working with watercolors, which are usually applied from top to bottom. An adjustable angle base is available separate from the board, which is made by Adjusto-Stand.

1.21 T-Square

Available in wood, steel, aluminum, or plastic, T-squares come with or without an inch (or other calibration) scale. The square should be at least as long as the drawing board on which it is used.

1.22 Triangles and Protractors

Available in a great variety of sizes and in 30/60° or 45° or adjustable degrees, they are used in combination with the T-square as well as in other ways. Available with inking edges and occasionally also with an inch or millimeter scale, they are produced in acrylic, aluminum, and steel.

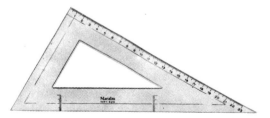

17

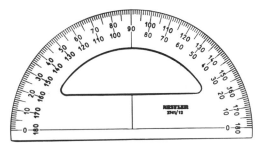

1.23 Rulers

They should be metal, plastic, or a similar stable material, have inch and pica scales, and be 12″, 18″, or 24″ long. An inking edge is also very handy.

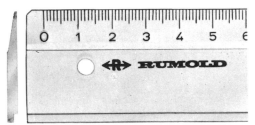

1.24 Cutting Straight Edge

Use this for cutting mats, paper, and board. It is available either in all steel, acrylic with steel inset, or in aluminum with a steel inset against which the cutting is done. There should be a rubber or cork strip on the bottom or back so that the straight edge cannot slip during cutting.

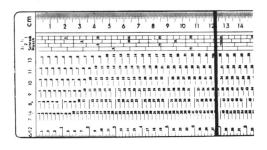

1.25 Type Gauge Ruler

This is a typographical measuring stick for copyfitting type sizes from 6 to 15 points and a scale for type pica lines.

1.26 French Curves

These are available with a wide variety of curves, such as hyperboles, parabolas, and ellipses, for use in drawing curves accurately.

18

1.27 Circle and Ellipse Templates

These serve—like French curves—as aids in drawing. They can also be used as templates for spraying if the holes not desired are covered up.

1.28 Drafter's Brush

Use this to sweep eraser crumbs and other debris from the work table and the work itself.

1.29 Blending Stumps *(Estompes)*

Paper sticks pointed at one or both ends are used for blending pencil, charcoal, and pastels.

2 Color

2.0 Colored Pencils

These wooden pencils are available in the following brands: Stabilo, Verithin, Prismacolor (waterproof), Faber-Castell, Caran d'Ache. Col-Erase pencils by Faber-Castell are the hardest. They can be sharpened to a very fine point and do not get dull quickly. Stabilo "All" Pencils can be used as drawing chalk, as colored pencils, and, since they are water soluble, as watercolors. They are also legible on any glazed surface (metal, photo film, plastic, acetate).

2.1 Colored Leads for Mechanical Pencils

There is a wide range of brands: Castell TK color is water soluble and comes in 17 shades. Koh-I-Noor color is available in 24 shades and is water soluble; these leads require a special pencil because they are thicker than others. Turquoise drawing leads No. BEL come in 11 shades.

2.2 Pastel Color Sticks

These intense colors are normally used over a colored background; they require the use of a fixative. Brands include: Alphacolor, Cray-Pas, Grumbacher, Hi-Fi, Nupastel.

2.3 Oil Crayons

Like pastel color sticks but on an oil base, oil crayons come in a wide choice of colors; you do not need a fixative. One brand is Cray-Pas. They are soluble in turpentine or gasoline (lighter fluid).

2.4 Other Chalk and Charcoal Sticks

Pastel pencils are actually chalk, and are not water soluble. Faber-Castell makes Carb-Othello pencils in a wide variety of colors. Other chalk sticks include blending sticks, charcoal, red clay sticks, and wax painting sticks.

2.5 Felt-Tipped Markers

Since there are innumerable brands of markers in very different price ranges, no specific products will be mentioned here. However, there are markers with:

1. Water-soluble ink that can then be painted over to some extent with water.
2. Alcohol ink; this is not water soluble, but it can be painted over with a special thinner for alcohol-base inks.
3. Reflective ink, that is, Day-Glo. Note that marker colors will deteriorate to some degree if exposed to light.
4. Metallic ink including gold, silver, copper.

2.6 Watercolors

Available in tablet and tube form in over 100 shades; watercolors by definition are not waterproof. Brands include Grumbacher and Winsor & Newton.

2.7 Gouache (Designers' Colors)

Available in tubes, gouache is brilliant in tone, opaque, and not waterproof. Used like tempera, it can also be used as a primer for oils.

2.8 Opaque Watercolors

Available in only a few shades, opaque watercolors (marabu designers' colors) are sold in tablet form in boxes and are cheaper than other watercolors. Most useful in laying out preliminary color sketches, these paints are not waterproof.

2.9 Tempera

Water-soluble tempera is available in tubes or jars. It is very similar to gouache, but not as fine and therefore less expensive. RichArt poster tempera offers 23 shades and is not waterproof.

2.10 Retouching Colors

In tablets and tubes, matte or shiny, and water soluble, retouching colors are usually used in airbrushes for retouching color prints. These colors, which are not waterproof, are also suitable for spraying on paper or board.

2.11 Casein (Plaka)

Available in tubes and can, casein is mixed with water, and once dry, it is waterproof.

2.12 Resin-Base Latex Paint

Mixed with water, it becomes waterproof when dry. This paint, available in cans and plastic jars, is used primarily for mixing and blending colors for the building industry, but it can also be used like casein or acrylic paint.

2.13 Acrylic Paint

Packaged in tubes, this paint is applied with water but is waterproof when dry. It looks like oil paint but is much easier to use and dries very quickly. When mixed with a retarder, it can be applied like oils. The number of shades is limited. Liquitex offers 30: 12 transparent, 18 opaque; Aquatec offers 34.

2.14 Liquitex and Aquatec Acrylic Mediums

There are a number of additives that produce different effects in acrylic paints: one for layering; ones that produce matte or shiny surfaces; one that permits application in relief; a varnish; and a retarder.

2.15 Oil Paint

Oils offer the widest range of colors and are waterproof when dry. Packaged in tubes, the pigments are mixed with oil painting mediums and are not water soluble.

2.16 Oil Painting Mediums and Varnishes

Here, too, there are various varnishes, underpaints, and glazing mediums that permit faster or slower drying and produce a matte or shiny surface. Various varnishes and primers are also available.

2.17 Alkyd Paints

Oil paints with an alkyd-resin base; they dry very quickly and evenly. They can be mixed with normal oil mediums as well as with the special mediums Liquin and Win-Gel. Brands include: Griffin by Winsor & Newton; 34 colors available in tubes.

2.18 Primer

Available commercially as Gesso, primer can be used for underpainting surfaces like linen or wood. It can also be used for both acrylic and oil paints.

2.19 Liquid Aniline Watercolors (Dyes)

Packaged in bottles with droppers, liquid aniline watercolors can be thinned with water for application, but are not waterproof when dry and will fade somewhat when exposed to light. Available brands include Dr. Ph. Martin's Radiant and Synchromatic Watercolors and Luma Liquid Watercolors, which can be used to color photographs.

2.20 Dr. Ph. Martin's Color Remover

Since the liquid watercolors are aniline paints, they can be removed (though sometimes only partially) with laundry bleach. Manufacturers of watercolors offer small jars of "color remover," but household bleach is cheaper.

2.21 Opaque White for Liquid Watercolors

Available as a liquid opaque white (Dr. Martin's Bleedproof White or Luma Designers' White), it is also useful to prevent bleeding colors. It can also be used to cover marker colors and bleeding colors. Apply again after dry, if necessary.

2.22 Photo Ace by Dr. Martin

Liquid medium in bottles and with a dropper, used with Dr. Martin's dyes. It aids in their "biting into" photo gel emulsions on film or prints.

23

2.23 Waterproof Colored Inks

Sold in cartridges, jars, and bottles, these drawing inks can be diluted with distilled or boiled water but become waterproof when dry. Eighteen colors are available in Pelikan Waterproof Drawing Inks No. KRI.

2.24 Color System

The Pantone Matching System includes felt-tipped markers, colored papers, colored overlay films (both solid color and screens), ColorKey films, and Letrachrome Imaging and dry transfer printer's inks, all cross-numbered for easy reference. The colors in the different media correspond to each other so that the colors in the final printing will be identical with the ones used in the mock-up or sketch or specified by number from a color swatch book.

2.25 Fixative

Packaged in bottles and spray cans, this is used to protect work in pencil, colored pencil, or pastels. These are various fixatives for different surfaces— Crystal Clear, Workable fixative, and Matte Finish. Hair spray can also be used.

2.26 Film Opaque Brush-On Ink

A red-brown retouching ink for film and acetate, it comes in a jar or tube. The brown tone is photographically opaque and the correction optically visible. It is most commonly used as a marker.

3 Papers and Boards

3.0 Typing Paper

Regular $8^{1}/_{2}'' \times 11''$ typing paper in reams is the handiest and cheapest sketching paper one can buy. However, the quality of typing paper varies greatly; for use with pen and ink or felt-tipped markers, a smooth-surfaced paper is essential otherwise lines will blot and run.

3.1 Layout and Visualizing Paper

This partially transparent paper is good for sketching, particularly with felt tipped markers. The paper does not bleed through and is available in pads measuring $9'' \times 12''$, $11'' \times 14''$, $14'' \times 17''$, and $19'' \times 24''$.

3.2 Tracing Paper

This paper comes in sheets, pads, and rolls. A handy size for sketching is the 14" x 50-yard roll [35.5-cm x 45-meter]. Other sizes are the 36" (91.4-cm) roll [50 yards (45 meters)] and the 42" (106.7-cm) roll (50 yards). A special tracing paper containing polyester is dimensionally stable. Vellum paper is strong, smooth, and supertranslucent, it takes pen and ink, is available in regular and heavy weight, and comes in the same sizes as tracing paper.

3.3 Light- and Heavy-Weight Bond Paper

This is available in pads measuring $9'' \times 12''$, $11'' \times 14''$, $14'' \times 17''$, $19'' \times 24''$, $24'' \times 36''$ and in both smooth and fine-grained surfaces.

3.4 Bristol Boards

Available in 1, 2, 3, 4, or 5 ply, Bristol boards usually measure $23'' \times 29''$ or $30'' \times 40''$. Both vellums and smooth surfaces are sold; vellum Bristol board is a particularly good surface for watercolors, while the smooth is excellent for all pen-and-ink work.

3.5 Mat Boards and/or Mounting Boards

These boards are used for layout and paste-up and come in 6, 14, and 28 ply. Sizes range from $23'' \times 29''$ to $40'' \times 60''$.

3.6 Exhibit Board

An extremely light polystyrene foam that is sandwiched between high-quality paperboard liner facings. For mounting layouts, pho-

tos, posters, etc., for presentations or exhibits. Available in
$32'' \times 40''$ and $24'' \times 36''$, $^3/_{16}''$ or $^1/_8''$ thick. From Monsanto or
Charrette.

3.7 Cross-Section Graph Paper

Printed both sides in nonreproducible blue ink on a strong, durable
white stock, this paper is available in 4×4, 5×5, 6×6, 8×8,
10×10 squares to the inch. Because the grid will not reproduce in
photocopies, this paper is useful for montages and technical drawings.

3.8 Painting Boards

The surface of this heavy cardboard is structured to take watercolors, acrylic paints, and oils; it is also available in laminated canvas.

4 Colored Papers

4.0 Heavy Bristol Boards

Ideal for mats, montages, and models, these heavy boards come in
mat weights of 1 to 5 ply and in sizes $23'' \times 29''$ and $30'' \times 40''$.
They are not recommended for color sketches because the surface is
not hard enough and is easily torn by Scotch or masking tape.

4.1 Watercolor Papers and Boards

Sheets, boards, pads, and blocks are available in white with the
following surfaces: R=rough, HP=hot pressed, and CP=cold
pressed. Brands include Strathmore, D'Arches, Fabriano Classico.

4.2 Handmade Watercolor Paper

Most often this paper is available in sheets, but sometimes also in
pads. This expensive white and colored paper is especially made for
watercolors, pastels, colored pencil, and gouache. Two brands are
Fabriano and D'Arches.

4.3 Colored Mat Board

Used mostly for mounting and collages, it is also useful for certain
kinds of work in colored pencil or pastels. It is sold in sheets and
comes in several finishes (smooth, pebble, and fabric-covered).

4.4 Tinted Paper

Sold in sheets, thinner than mat board but similar in its uses.

4.5 Color-Aid Paper

Sold in sheets, it can be worked with airbrush, colored pencils, pastels, tempera, ink, casein, and acrylic paint. It is available in 220 coordinated colors: 24 basic blues, 4 tints and 3 shades of each line, 16 grays, black, and white.

4.6 Pantone Colored Paper by Letraset

Available in sheets of 505 colors, it was described under Color System above. It can be worked in most of the ways Color-Aid paper can, but it is not as stable with wet media.

4.7 Other Colored Papers and Boards

Grandee (80 lb. text papers), Beau Brilliant (65 lb. cover stock), Strathmore (No. STCS cover stock), Strathmore Charcoal, Multicolor Antique, Mi-Teintes Tinted, Colorcast Flint, Fantasia (cover stock) are some of the brand names on the market.

5 Acetates

5.0 Clear and Matte Acetates

Available in sheets and rolls, which are to some degree dimensionally stable, acetates are useful for drawing mechanicals, animated film, overlays, and montages. Prepared acetates will take inks, tempera, casein, and acrylic paint, although it is always advisable to make a trial run before using any product on a finished piece of work. Pencils and colored pencils can also be used on frosted or matte acetate. Brands include Clear Acetate (No. SPAC), Frosted (Semi-Matte Acetate (No. SPAP), Prepared Acetate (No. SPAPP), Cello-Tak (Transparent) Frisket, Copyzip Adhesive Clear Film (Zipatone).

5.1 Color Overlays or Color/Tint Overlays

These come in sheets with adhesive backs. Brands include Pantone Color/Tint Overlays by Letraset (more than 217 colors), which is described above under Color System; Zipatone shading Films and Color Overlay Sheets (142 colors); and Cello-Tak Color Film-Transparent Color Overlays (230 colors).

5.2 Screens and Pattern Overlays

Sheets with adhesive backs are available in many patterns, such as lines, dots, and screen progressions, some of which can be transferred by rubbing. Some brands sold are Letraset Letratone and Zipatone Shading Films, Screens, and Patterns.

5.3 Transfer Material/Transfer Lettering

Available in innumerable typefaces, textures, and symbols, it is applied by rubbing with a sharp point. Brands include Letraset Instant Lettering, Tactype, Letragraphic Instant Sheets.

5.4 Frisket Paper and Friskfilm

Frisket paper comes in sheets or rolls, is lightly adhesive, and is used for painting, spraying, and stipple brushwork. Adhesive can be cleaned with a rubber cement pick-up. Available in 24" x 15' roll, matte finish. Friskfilm is a low-tack, soft-peel masking film with a translucent backing paper. Can be used as protective overlay in addition to masking and matte finish will accept pencil. Available in rolls and sheets.

5.5 Masking Film

Useful for blocking out areas on mechanicals and artwork overlays to be used for camera work, these films come on acetate backing in rolls or sheets. The red film reacts in the camera as black; otherwise it is transparent so you can see through and cut out what has to be eliminated.) Rubylith and Amerlith are the leading brands.

6 Implements for Painting and Other Procedures

6.0 Watercolor Brushes/Round with Fine Point

The well-known brands include Winsor & Newton, Albata Series 7 (sizes 000 to 14); Grumbacher Series 197 (sizes 000 to 14); Art and Sign Series 9 (sizes 000 to 12) and Series 872 (sizes 00 to 6).

6.1 Watercolor Brushes/Flat

Grumbacher Series 40 (sizes 2 to 10) is one of the brands on the market.

6.2 Retouching Brushes

Winsor & Newton Series WN 3A (sizes 000 to 8) and Grumbacher Series 178 (sizes 00000 to 5) are very useful for fine work in acrylics.

6.3 Bristle Brushes/Round and Flat

Synthetic fiber is ideal for flat surfaces in casein and acrylic. Simmons Series SI 40, Rounds, Flats, Brights (sizes 0 to 12) is the primary brand.

6.4 Varnish Brushes

These brushes are specially made for varnishing oil or acrylic paints and also for painting flat surfaces in casein and acrylics. Brands include Grumbacher White Bristle Cutters, Series 8966 (sizes 1″ to 3″); Golden Nylon Acrylic Brushes (TARA) (sizes 1″ to 3″).

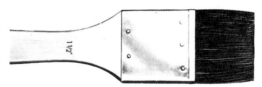

6.5 Stipple or Stencil Brushes

These are needed for stenciling with tempera, casein, acrylics, and oils. Grumbacher Series 1131 (sizes 2 to 12) is a commonly used brand.

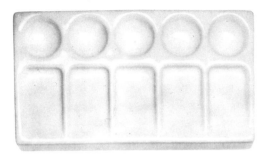

6.6 Palettes

For watercolors, tempera, gouache, and acrylics, porcelain palettes with both round and rectangular depressions are best. For oils and acrylics there are, in addition to wooden and plastic palettes, throw-away palettes made of special paper.

6.7 Spatulas and Palette Knives

These are useful for mixing colors on a palette or on glass; they can also be used for spatula work.

6.8 Utility Knives

1. This knife uses replaceable blades; it is essential for cutting boards and other thick materials. Brands include Stanley or SurGrip by X-Acto.

2. This knife has a segmented blade, so segments can be broken off when dull. NT Cutter Multi-Edge Knives and JETRIC Cutter Knives JE 100 are 2 brands.

3. X-Acto knives and blades come with a variety of handles and a wide choice of blades, suitable for cutting, scraping, and other uses.

6.9 Swivel Knife

Available with a ball-bearing mounted, swivel blade, it is useful for cutting curves and circles in acetate. Brands are Grifhold and X-Acto.

6.10 Scissors

You will need scissors for all paper-cutting work. Fiskars and Wiss are among the most frequently used brands.

6.11 Silhouette Scissors

These special scissors are needed for finely detailed work.

6.12 Single-Edged Razor Blade

This is the most versatile and frequently used cutting tool.

6.13 Arkansas Oilstone

This is useful for sharpening knives, and blades.

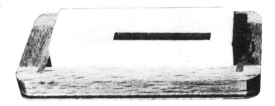

6.14 Burnishers

This tool is needed for smoothing the edges of board, for folding paper, and for burnishing transfer material.

6.15 Reducing Glass

This is a useful tool for judging drafts that are larger than the final product will be or for seeing how a poster will look at a distance.

6.16 Magnifier Loupe and Linen Testers

These items are frequently needed to examine photo negatives, slides, contacts, and other very small material. Agta 8X is one brand available.

6.17 Stand Magnifier

This magnifying glass is for very small, detailed work that cannot be done with the naked eye.

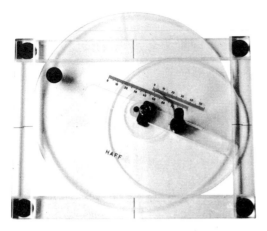

6.18 Ellipsograph

This device for drawing ellipses up to $6^{3}/_{4}"$ x $4^{1}/_{4}"$ (170 x 110 mm) uses a lead pencil insert; a technical pen can also be used.

6.19 Cross-Hatching Machine

This is useful for drawing straight or curved line textures and patterns. A French curve can be inserted, and the device can be adjusted to any setting.

6.20 Proportion Disk (Proportional Scale Disk)

This is used for sealing artwork and determining percentages of reduction or enlargement of photo and picture formats. Like a slide rule in principle, it is in fact easier to use.

6.21 Airbrushes

These are needed for producing fine color hues, retouching, creating smooth color shading.

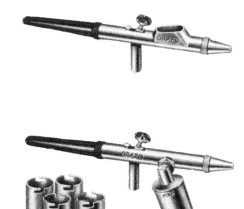

1. Paasch Airbrushes come in a few models: V-1 for fine detail and V-2 for faster coverage. Model F-1 runs at slower speed for beginners; Model H can produce a wide range of color effects; and Model VL is the most versatile.

2. Thayer and Chandler Airbrushes have Models A and AA. Various parts and attachments are available for both brands.

6.22 Compressors, Regulators, and Tanks for Airbrushes

Airbrushes run off a compressor, are portable, and can be plugged into any electrical outlet. They can also be operated off tanks of propellant gas or CO_2 cylinders, but for either of these alternatives a regulator is also required. Compressor brands include Sprayit and Paasche.

6.23 Opaque Projector

A device for vertical and horizontal projections of nontransparent art, this very powerful projector can enlarge and reduce originals. The original can be projected directly onto the material where it can then be traced or worked up in some other way. Two brands are Artograph Vertical Opaque Projector and Kopyrite Opaque Projector.

6.24 Lucy (Lucigraph)

This device is used for tracing enlarged or reduced art from opaque and three-dimensional materials and objects as well as from transparent materials such as slides or other film. The enlargement or reduction is projected onto the glass plate on top and drawn onto tracing paper, vellum, drafting paper, or prepared acetate. One brand, Goodkin, comes in several models: Model A Viewer, Swivel-Top Projector, Model 5B Viewer.

6.25 Contact Copying Machine

A less known copier than the more popular dry machines, such as by Xerox and Canon, nevertheless exceedingly useful for the graphic artist. Consists of an exposure unit and a built-in developing device. For more information, see pages 211, 218–219. Leading brand is Agfa-Gevaert Copyrapid Offset F13.

7 Adhesives

7.0 Glues

All-purpose glues such as Duco Cement, Sobo, and Elmer's Glue-All are a must in any studio.

7.1 Rubber Cement

Packaged in cans, jars, and bottles with a brush attached to the lid, this is a strong, natural, white rubber adhesive used for mounting photographs, paper, or lines of type. Depending on the quality of the paper used, layouts glued with rubber cement can be separated again with rubber cement thinner. One disadvantage is that rubber cement will degenerate in time and cause stains.

7.2 Rubber Cement Thinner

Packaged in cans, this is excellent for thinning rubber cement that has gotten too thick to work with easily. Adding too much, however, will thin the cement and make it lose its adhesive quality. Evaporates easily; is highly flammable.

7.3 Rubber Cement Pick-Up

A piece of raw rubber can be used for quick removal and pick-up of excess dry cement and of transfer lettering.

7.4 Aerosol Spray Adhesives

Sold in cans, these are used for mounting artwork, type, acetate, and large format paper and board.

7.5 Wax

This adhesive is used for mechanicals and other types of nonpermanent adhesion. The advantage is that it will adhere longer than rubber cement. Must be applied with a special machine.

7.6 Tapes

These come in a multitude of variations: transparent, frosted, crepepaper, plastic, paper, foam, linen, colored. The primary brand is 3M's Scotch.

7.7 Double-Coated Tapes and Adhesive Materials

Sold in rolled sheets and tapes, these are useful for mounting photos and paper and working with templates. Several brands are Scotch, Seal, Instant Twin Mount, and Rubber cement tape.

7.8 Dry Mount

This is a process of mounting photos or paper on board with dry mounting adhesive tissues, using a tacking iron or dry-mounting press.

8 Special Papers

8.0 Graphite Paper

This paper, similar to carbon paper but coated with the graphite used in pencil leads, is used for transferring a tracing onto another working surface. The lines it makes can be erased. One brand is Saral.

8.1 Chalk Paper

This is used to transfer tracings onto dark backgrounds, because the lines it makes can be erased. It comes in several colors.

8.2 Copyproof Materials for the Contact Copy Processor

CPC Negative paper
CPP Positive paper
CP 296 B Developer
CP 297 B Higher-density developer (CPF)

8.3 Copyproof Materials for Repro Cameras

CPN Negative paper for high-contrast negative
CPRV Right-reading, high-contrast negative paper
CPTN Negative paper for halftone work
These negative materials have to be used, together with the positives, under a red darkroom light.

CPP Positive paper
CPPm Matte positive paper
CPG Glossy positive paper
CPF Positive film available in thicknesses of .10 and .05 mm
CPFm Matte positive film, .10 mm thick

The positive paper and the clear positive film can also be had with self-adhering coating on the back (CPP AB and CPF AB). These positive materials can be exposed to light.

CP 296 B developer, recommended temperature 70°F. $\pm$ 3°F. If you want a higher-density black in your positives, you have to use the developer CP 297 B with the combination CPN + CPF/CPFm.

8.4 ColorKey Overlays

These photosensitive overlays are available in 41 transparent and 10 opaque shades and must be used with a special developer. White can be colored over with water soluble markers.

8.5 Chromatec Transfers

This is a process for making your own black or colored friction-transfer elements. For more information, see pages 264–267.

8.6   Letrachrome Dry Transfer

As with Chromatec, this is also a process for making black or colored friction-transfer elements. For information, see pages 261–264.

8.7   Letrachrome Direct Imaging

By exposing layers to ultraviolet light, you can create the impression of a finished print, and can make prints on white paper or transparencies on clear acetate. For more information, see pages 252–258.

Graphic Translation of a Photograph into a Line Drawing

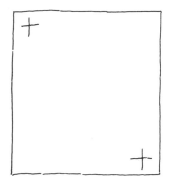

Graphite paper 8.0

Many of the examples shown in this book are graphic translations of photographs. Instead of working from a real object, the artist has copied a print or a photograph in a book or magazine.

To do this, he or she uses a thin pencil to draw 2 to 4 register marks on the original. Register marks are simply crosses about half an inch long. They are always used whenever several colors or parts have to be laid one over the other in exactly the same position. Using these register marks, an artist can reposition tracing paper quickly and accurately on the original if it has been taken off for some reason or if it has accidentally slipped.

The artist then lays a sheet of highly transparent tracing paper or vellum over the original and fastens it in place with pieces of masking tape on either side. He or she then traces the register marks on the tracing paper and, using a hard, sharp pencil (2H to 4H), starts carefully and lightly tracing the outlines, the inner details, and the shaded areas. Note that lines drawn with a *soft* pencil quickly broaden and are easily smudged, with the result that the contour line details can soon be obscured in the original.

Once all the contours have been traced, the drawing can be transferred to paper, board, canvas, or any other surface. This can be done in one of 2 ways. The tracing paper or vellum is fastened to the new surface with masking tape. Then a piece of graphite paper is slipped under the tracing paper, and a hard, sharp pencil is used to trace over the contours on the tracing paper. Varying degrees of pressure are required, depending on the material to which the tracing is being transferred. Care must be taken not to tear the tracing paper. The lines left by the graphite paper can be erased. Ordinary typewriter carbon paper should not be chosen for this purpose because the lines smear if they are erased. If you need to transfer lines onto a dark background, use a chalk paper, which will leave erasable white lines.

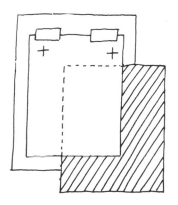

If you do not have any graphite paper, you can use another, somewhat more complicated method. Turn over the tracing paper or vellum with the drawing on it, and go over all the contour lines with a soft pencil. Then lay the drawing right side up on the new surface and trace over the lines again with a hard pencil. The transferred contour lines will often be wide and blurred, so it is a good idea to go over them once again with a hard pencil. Finally, go over the entire drawing lightly with an eraser to get rid of the excess pencil lead. A sharp, clear line from the hard pencil is all that should remain visible.

Photographs often have so little contrast that contours and shadings disappear when tracing paper is laid over them. This makes a precise line conversion difficult. In such cases, use a thin, transparent acetate instead of tracing paper and trace the contours with a fine technical pen (.18, .25, or .35 mm). To ensure that the lines adhere to the acetate, wipe the acetate with a paper towel soaked in soap suds. If the acetate is thin enough, the tracing can now be transferred onto paper or board with graphite paper as described above, or you can make a tracing paper tracing from the acetate and use that to transfer the contour lines to the paper or board.

Acetates 5.0

Technical pen 1.10

The Preliminary Drawing as a Transfer Tracing

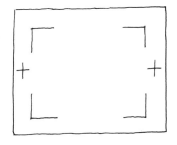

All the preliminary sketches and studies that you make for your final design should be consolidated into one preliminary drawing that can serve as a work drawing for transferring the design onto the final surface. This is a simple line drawing on tracing paper; it includes all the contours and details in the *same size* in which they will appear in your finished design and can therefore be directly transferred onto the final material by one of the methods described in the preceding section.

If you are working on paper or board, you should always leave sufficient margins to be covered later by your mat or for trimming. These margins should be shown on your preliminary drawings, too, in the form of a continuous line around the working area, or you can simply put 4 right angles or register marks in the corners of the tracing to line it up on your working material.

Before you can begin painting, stippling, or spraying, trace the largest areas and backgrounds onto your working material and color them in. Then trace the next largest objects and surfaces, finishing with the smallest details. If you tried to transfer the entire tracing onto the working material at one time using opaque paints, for example, you would find it impossible to overlay colors. This would not be the case, of course, if you were using watercolors, where pencil lines remain visible, or if you applied opaque colors in fields that never overlapped.

You may want to make changes in your composition in the course of your work. Let's assume, for example, that in the picture shown on the left, you want to change the position of the tree. All you have to do is move your tracing paper slightly to the left and trace the tree in its new position. In this way, you can spare yourself having to redo the entire preliminary drawing.

Pencil Drawing

The pencil is one of the oldest, cheapest, most popular, and most universal of drawing instruments. Sharpening is the only preparation it requires, and the only other things you need for pencil drawing, in addition to pencil and paper, are an eraser and a pencil sharpener.

With a pencil, you can do everything from the simplest doodlings to the most sophisticated, realistic drawings. It is an indispensable sketching medium because it is quick and uncomplicated. With the shading technique I describe here, you will be able to simulate photographic effects quickly and simply because the pencil is able to produce the same tones that a black and white photo can, ranging all the way from white through every shade of gray to black.

Many artists of the realistic school usually use fairly hard pencils, which can be made to produce, through repeated crosshatching, even the darkest of shadings. Drawings of this kind consist of innumerable tiny strokes that, taken together, create the impression of smooth transitions and progressions. Its only drawback is that a very large drawing may take months to complete by this method.

The type of pencil you use for this work is not crucial. But it pays to buy a few mechanical pencils if you intend to do a lot of drawing. The leads can be sharpened to a very fine point, and a lead sharpener that can be fastened to your table top is therefore a worthwhile investment. Note, however, that the smaller models are less practical.

Mechanical pencil 1.2

Lead sharpener 1.4

A page from *The Garden of Abdul Gasazi,* published by Houghton Mifflin Co., Boston, 1979. This picture book by Chris van Allsburg is done entirely with pencils, grades H-H10.

42

Blending

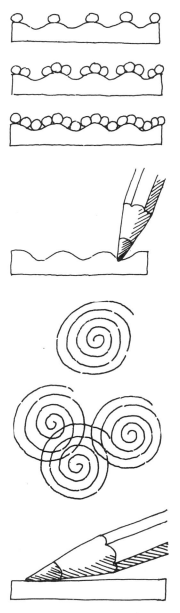

With blending, you can create highly realistic and 3-dimensional effects with pencils, crayons, chalks, and charcoal. The important thing is that the transitions in this kind of shading should flow and not show any border.

In blending, you are rubbing the pencil against the paper rather than drawing on it. As you rub, only the surface of the paper (or board) takes on the shading. The low spots and pores remain white. With repeated rubbing and increased pressure, the shading reaches the middle layers, and the most intense black is achieved by pressing still harder on the pencil or angling it down into the pores. The less structure the paper has, the more intense the shading can be. However, you should take care to use a *high-finish* drawing paper (for example, Bristol board) so that the pencil will not tear the surface or the surface become unable to absorb any more coloration. It is always a good idea, when doing pencil or colored pencil drawings, to test your pencils first on the paper you intend to use.

Hold the pencil flatter than you would for drawing and make spiral movements with it. These should be light and without pressure at first. Darker shades can be produced by repeated interlocking spirals. Make it a principle to begin very carefully and delicately with the light areas. Then move on slowly to the darker ones and finish up with the deepest shadows. The bright areas should be left untouched.

If you want to produce large shaded surfaces, lay the pencil point almost flat on the paper and move it lightly back and forth. In this way, you can produce flowing transitions and avoid linear borders.

Successful blending requires considerable patience because you have to work with the utmost care to avoid

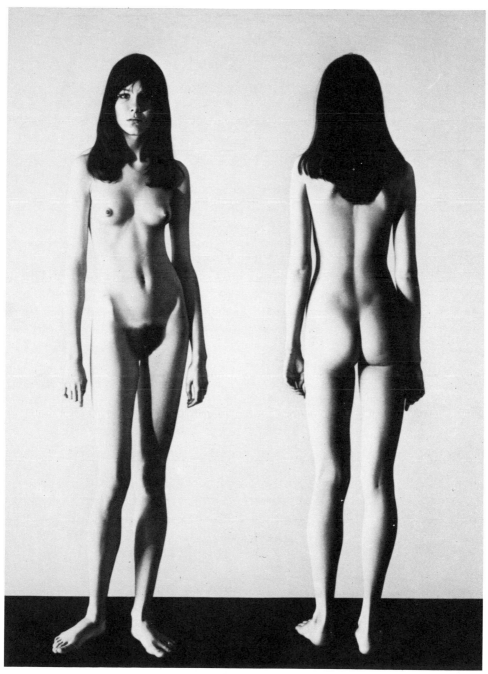

Claudio Bravo, "Eve" (from "Eve and Adam"). Pencil drawing, ca. 69″ x 49″ (174 x 123 cm). This life-sized drawing was done stroke by stroke. There is no blending in it.

smudging with these soft pencils. Place a sheet of paper under your drawing hand to keep the heel of your hand from smearing your work. If you want to make your transitions more subtle still, go over them again with Blending stump 1.29 paper or leather blending stumps. Hold the stumps like pencils and apply to the paper at either a steep or shallow angle to grind the graphite or colored powder further into the pores of the paper.

Light areas can be created with an eraser. Since there will often be quite small areas or angles that you have accidentally blended over, you can cut out a template in the shape of the light area. (Use vellum paper or an acetate that is neither too thick nor too thin so that the template will not tear or have high edges.) Lay the template in the proper place and erase lightly over it until you have the degree of brightness you want. Art supply stores also carry erasing templates made of thin tin with various shapes stamped out of them, if you prefer.

To prevent smudging of your finished work, apply a Fixative 2.25 fixative or hair spray, which is a much cheaper substitute. However, once you have done this, you *cannot do any further erasing* unless you use a special workable fixative.

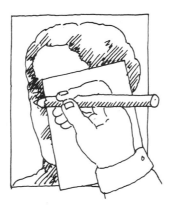

46

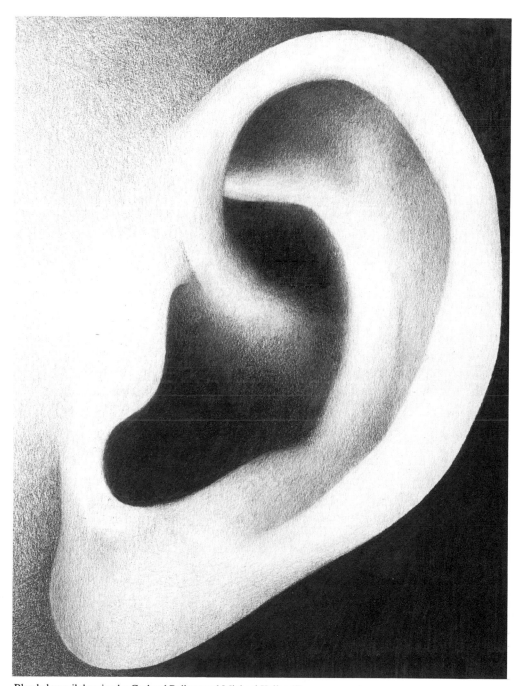

Blended pencil drawing by Gerhard Beikert and Michael Keller (S).

45° Rapid Shading

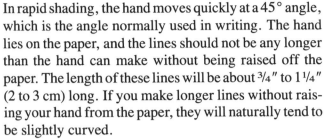

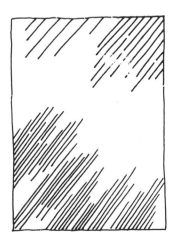

In rapid shading, the hand moves quickly at a 45° angle, which is the angle normally used in writing. The hand lies on the paper, and the lines should not be any longer than the hand can make without being raised off the paper. The length of these lines will be about ³/₄″ to 1¹/₄″ (2 to 3 cm) long. If you make longer lines without raising your hand from the paper, they will naturally tend to be slightly curved.

Now let's go over all the steps in a rapid shading. Put register marks on a photograph, then lay a highly transparent tracing paper over it, and secure it with 2 strips of masking tape. Starting in the upper left-hand corner, draw parallel lines over the shaded parts of the photo. Leave the white parts either completely untouched or shade them only very lightly. The first shading lines should be very light, showing no contrast between light and dark shading in the original. To check for contrast, slide a piece of white paper between the tracing paper and the photo.

Now go over the darker sections of the original with a second shading, pressing harder on the pencil or making the lines fall closer together or over each other. Keep checking the contrast with the aid of the white paper until the darkest areas on your tracing paper are analogous to those on the original. The darkest areas will thus be completed only at the end of your work and will have the greatest density of lines. Whether the drawing will have strong contrasts will depend on your intentions. A pale pencil conversion, poor in contrasts, can have its charm, too.

In shading, you should maintain all your lines at the same angle within the same drawing because this uniformity of angle will give your work stylistic unity.

Steps in working up 45°-rapid shading, by Maria Kohl (S). The first, gray layer of strokes is gone over and over until the desired degree of contrast is reached.

45°-rapid shading by Volkmar Hoppe (S).

45°-rapid shading by Elke Israng (S). ▷

45°-rapid shading (F - 3H mechanical pencil leads on Ingres paper) by Michael Keller,
preliminary study for a competition.

There is no need to change grades of pencils during your work. Most of the examples shown here were done with pencils of only one grade. In rapid shading, the style should be free. Portrait details like eyelashes or small wrinkles should simply be omitted; it is too fussy a job, for example, to draw an eyelash requiring 30 strokes only half an iota long. This procedure makes it possible, in a relatively short time, to recreate a photograph in a wide range of shades. Depending on the care taken in such drawing, you can use it as a rough sketch for layout purposes or as a finished drawing.

If possible, avoid using an eraser because the drawing can smear easily on tracing paper. Here, too, it is advisable to place a piece of protective paper under your drawing hand. Fix the finished work with hair spray or fixative.

Pen and Ink Drawing

Pen holder 1.6

Bond paper 3.3

For drawing, all you need is a simple wooden pen holder with an opening that will take a wide selection of broad and narrow nibs, ink, and a hard-surfaced paper. By trying different pens, you can find out before you begin your project which pen is best for you and the particular job you have in mind. If you want to draw with quick, strong lines, you may want a large writing or stenographer's pen that slides effortlessly over the paper and will produce a stronger line with an increase in pressure. If you want to do delicate work, you will

Pen point 1.7

want to choose a fine, hard pen point that has to be drawn across the paper with great care. Otherwise, a sharp point can catch and spray ink.

With enough care, you'll achieve excellent results even on rough board. For drawing, you can use all liquid media or media that can be made liquid, such as casein, ink, India ink, watercolors, and liquid aniline watercolors.

If you want to add watercolors to an ink drawing, you will have to use an ink that will not dissolve under the

Waterproof drawing ink 1.8

Waterproof colored ink 2.23

later application of the watercolors. India ink (waterproof drawing ink) is suitable for this purpose, but it becomes completely waterproof only after a long drying period, which can be as much as 24 hours or more. Therefore, you should always make a test before going

Black drawing ink 1.9

Drawing ink for technical pens 1.11

ahead with watercolor. Other black but not waterproof inks are Koh-I-Noor and Rapidograph inks.

Many drafters prefer the brown tones of a medium like sepia. If the ink drawing is to be filled in later with watercolors, the brown lines make the contrast between the colors and the drawing (which consists of contour lines, details within the contours, and shading) less drastic than with black ink. The final result is softer and more harmonious.

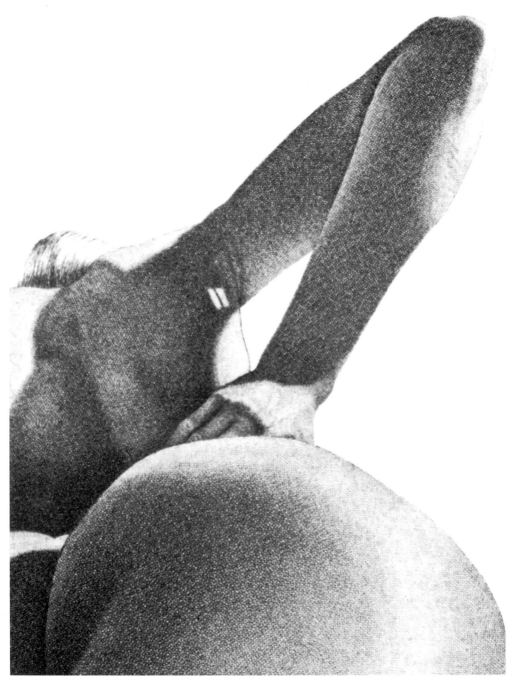

Section of a pen-and-ink drawing on board by Hartmut Lincke.

◁ Pen-and-ink drawing with crosshatching by Janice Hillman Shyles (S).

◁ In this pen-and-ink drawing, Edward Gorey uses shading to create a sense of light plasticity. The almost completely black areas of the ornaments contrast with the shading. From the book *The Blue Aspic*.

Pen-and-ink drawing using crosshatching with different spacings between the lines, by Chi-Ming Kan (S).   ▽

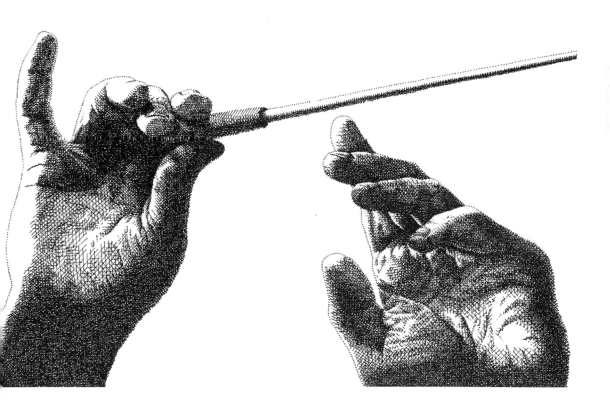

The angles used in shading and crosshatching patterns. The intensity of tone can be made lighter or darker by varying the width of the spaces between the lines.

90°   180°   90 + 180°

45°   135°   45 + 135°

45 + 90°
45 + 180°
45 + 90 + 180°

45 + 135 + 180°
45 + 90 + 135°
45 + 90 + 135 + 180°

Nineteenth-century American engraving. Curved lines used to be very popular in woodcuts and engravings. The curves followed the form of the body and gave it greater plasticity. These curved strokes are still used on banknotes. ▷

In this drawing of a fox (detail), Masayuki Yabuuchi uses very short pen strokes that represent both the shading of the body and the hairs in the fur. The pen strokes follow the direction of hair growth. ▽

Detail from the children's book *Higgelty Piggelty Pop!* Maurice Sendak uses very short and sometimes crooked pen strokes to create this mystical atmosphere. The figure of the little dog has no contour lines. The field around him marks the borderlines of his white fur.

Types of Shading

Shading is achieved with parallel lines that are drawn either freehand or with a ruler, and different shades of gray are represented with it. The closer together the lines, the darker the shade of gray will be until, finally, black (or if a color is being used, the full tone) is reached. Dark tones can be achieved by squeezing the lines together, by making them heavier, and by crossing them in what is called *crosshatching*. Making lines heavier is difficult to do in the process of drawing, and crosshatching with lines of equal thickness is a more reliable method. Crosshatching is also an essential technique in etching and engraving.

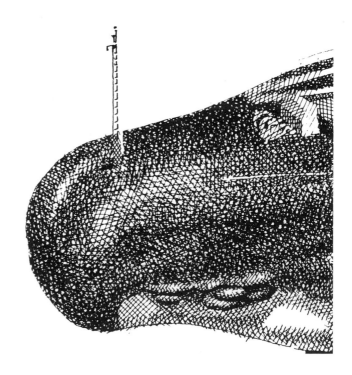

Two details from a pen-and-ink drawing by Yoshiro Amashita. These examples clearly illustrate the use of crosshatching done with varying intervals between the lines. The lines on the whale's head of the ship are only slightly curved. They hardly follow the body contour at all, but they still create a highly plastic effect. Different degrees of darkness are produced by crossing 2 or more lines. Notice how the directions of these lines, as well as the intervals between them, are varied.

Pen-and-ink drawing for the magazine *Eltern (Parents)*. Layout paper was placed over the 2-point perspective drawing. The artist then added the crosshatching on the layout paper using pen and ink.

Technical Pens

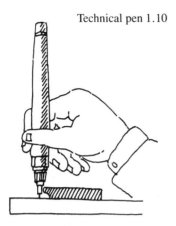

Technical pen 1.10

Technical pens are fountain pens with minute tubes as points. The diameters of the openings are standardized and range from .13 to 2.0 mm, or sizes 000 to 7. For each stroke width there is a separate pen tip. These pens are used primarily for technical and architectural drawing; here, in those drawings made with rulers, lines of different thicknesses have different meanings. Technical pens should be held as close to vertical as possible and drawn lightly, without pressure, along the ruler. Many drafters like to use technical pens for freehand drawing, too, because they are always ready for use. However, you have to use the special inks meant for these pens; otherwise, they will clog and be unusable.

Even if varying pressure is applied to a technical pen, the line produced will maintain a constant thickness. This makes drawings done with technical pens look somewhat sterile in comparison with regular pen-and-ink drawings in which the lines vary in thickness according to the pressure. After considerable use, particularly on rough papers, the tip of the pen becomes worn and no longer produces a stroke of the designated width. For this reason, do not use technical pens that have been used for freehand drawing to do precision technical drawing.

If a technical pen starts producing an irregular line, it is probably low on ink. Clean the tip in running water, dry it, and fill the pen's reservoir. Note that there are special colored inks available in a limited number of colors designed primarily for use in technical drawing.

Drawing ink for technical pens 1.11

Technical pens are ideal for making dots and dot shading. The tube point naturally produces an almost perfectly round dot, and one is spared the annoyance of having to dip the pen in ink during what is a tedious enough job in itself. To apply dots freehand, touch the

Portrait of Abdul Baha, done in dots with a technical pen, by Haynes and Rosann McFadden. The shading was done dot for dot, and it took the artists 200 hours to complete this work. This illustration shows only a detail from the picture (Scale: 1:1).

66

Detail of a bolt for a door by Don Stevenson (S). This work was done with a technical pen, too, and required 35 hours to complete.

Reduced drawings for a stamp competition. Since these drafts were supposed to be printed in only 2 colors, either by offset or engraving processes, they had to be executed in either lines or dots.

Drafts for postage stamps—as well as the final mechanicals—are ordinarily done on a scale 6 times larger than the finished work. Small imperfections then disappear in the reduction. Inexact beginnings of lines, as in the drawing on page 70, cause no problems at all in the later reduction. In the drawing on page 69, only 1 stroke width was used. The shadings are created by using crosshatching executed with different spacings between lines. In the drawing on page 70, however, technical pens with different sized strokes were used. The final step was to convert the line drawings into ColorKey (see page 248).

68

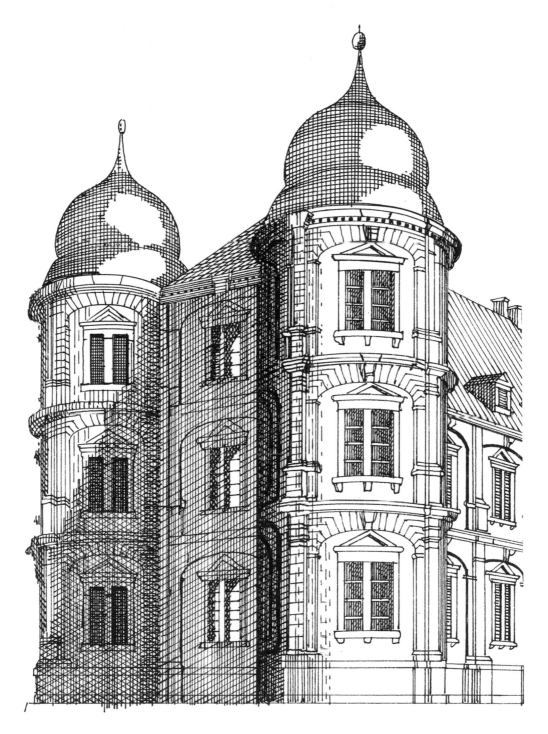

69

70

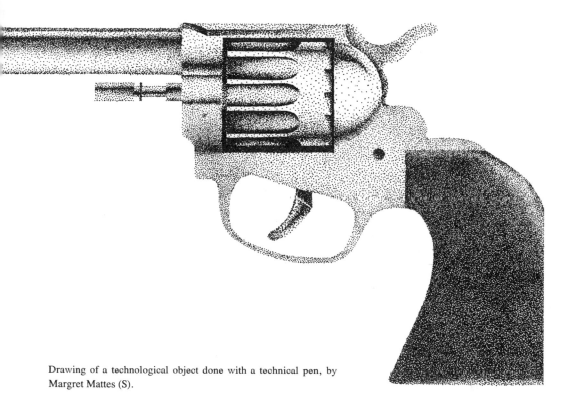

Drawing of a technological object done with a technical pen, by
Margret Mattes (S).

pen lightly to tracing paper or acetate laid over the original. As in shading, begin with the light gray areas, then proceed to the darker shadings.

To apply dots in a regular pattern, take a fine pencil and draw a grid on a piece of tracing paper. Ordinarily, the squares in the grid will measure $\frac{1}{8}''$ to $\frac{3}{16}''$ (3 to 5 mm), but the size of the squares can be adapted to suit your needs. Lay the tracing paper on the original with the grid side down. In white areas, do not put any dots on the line crossings. In light gray areas, make small dots; in darker ones, larger dots; and in black areas, the largest dots. When you are done, erase the pencil grid.

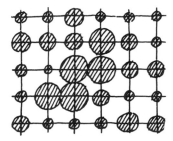

Line-screen effect, done manually by Greg Foster (S). In making this line pattern, the artist begins with thin lines that can then be widened as needed.

Dot-screen effect, done manually by Monika Rinke (S).

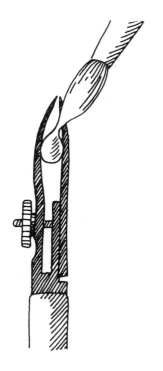

Ruling Pen (With Cross Joint)

The ruling pen, which was formerly used only for drawing ink lines along a ruler, has long since been made obsolete in technical drawing by the much more practical technical pens. However, the ruling pen still offers an advantage: You can apply any liquid or liquifiable color you like (watercolors, inks, gouache, tempera, casein, acrylics, and oils) with any kind of ruler, including French curves. This procedure can be used in any project requiring precise, colored borders—either straight or curved—for colored areas or wherever colored lines have to be drawn. The cross joint greatly facilitates cleaning the pen.

The Procedure

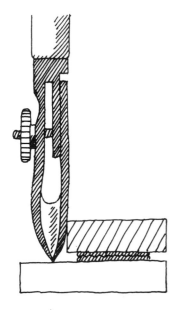

Dilute the paint in a small saucer until it is just thin enough to drop off a brush. Make some trial pen strokes to test if you have the proper consistency. If the paint flows out of the pen with difficulty, it has not been thinned enough. If it drips and spatters, it is too thin. Note that inks and liquid aniline watercolors can be applied unthinned.

Open the tip of the ruling pen about 1/32″ (1.5 mm) and fill the pen with the aid of a small brush. Screw the pen shut a little bit and make a trial stroke on a piece of paper. If the paint is the proper consistency, all you need do now is adjust the pen to make as thick or thin a stroke as you want. The stroke does not need to be very wide, for you can produce a broader line by adding as many parallel strokes to it as you like. However, it is a good idea to let the previously applied lines dry before adding any more. Since there is a danger of ink running under a ruler that does not have inking edges (and most French curves do not), add "feet" to the ruler by sticking 2 or more layers of masking tape to its underside.

A Practical Example

A rectangle is to be filled in with casein or acrylics. First, draw the outline with a 3H or 4H pencil. Use the ruling pen to trace over this line with the properly thinned paint. When this first line is dry, run a second one inside it so that the original one is now twice as wide. This procedure can be repeated as often as you like, but as a rule, a doubled or tripled line will do. Now, within this frame, apply the paint in a thicker consistency than that used in the ruling pen in a criss-cross pattern. Using a flat brush, apply a layer of paint horizontally; then, after that has dried, apply one vertically and so on until the surface is adequately covered.

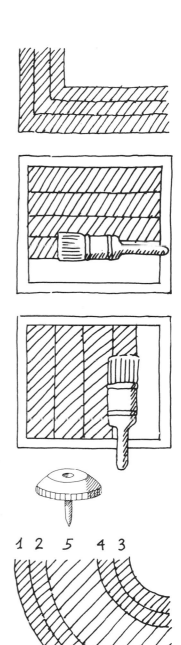

Another Example

A ring is to be filled in with paint. Replace the pencil insert in your compass with a ruling pen insert. Make a few trial circles on a piece of scrap paper. Any paint that is left sticking to the outside edge of the pen after filling. should be wiped off with a paper towel to prevent smearing.

First draw the ring with your pencil insert. Because you may have to stick your compass repeatedly in the center of the circle, use masking tape or another similar tape on the base of the compass (or a compass with a stepped point) to keep the compass point from enlarging the center hole and making it impossible to retrace your circle exactly. Now put your ruling pen into the compass, set the compass to the size of your circle, fill the pen, and trace the circle. To thicken the original line, add additional ones, working toward the inside. Thicken the inner line of your ring by adding lines working toward the outside. Finally, use a brush to fill in the space between the lines.

Felt-Tipped Markers

There are markers with fine, medium, and wide felt tips. Using the appropriate markers, you can quickly execute a wide variety of designs ranging from a fine line drawing to filling in a field of color.

The markers contain a felt tip that is soaked in colors which are either *water* soluble or *alcohol* soluble. Unfortunately, most of these colors are not light resistant, and they will fade if exposed to sunlight and even when they are kept in a drawer. Advertising agencies prefer the alcohol-soluble markers for layouts and presentations, not only because the range of colors available is very extensive and don't wrinkle the paper on which they are applied, but also because treating these colors with solvents can produce a certain realistic effect. Because such works are needed for a short time only, their vulnerability to light is of no consequence.

Procedure

Since felt-tipped markers are ready to use as they come out of the package, no complex preparations are needed. However, most of the colors are very bright, and if you want to produce subtle tones, you either have to have a very extensive set of markers or thin the colors with a solvent. Therefore, to produce a pale background, dip a paper towel in solvent, rub the towel over your paper, apply the color in strips with a broad-tipped marker, then wipe the whole surface down with the towel again. Remember, for marker work, you should use a good quality layout paper that will not bleed through.

Layout and visualizing paper 3.1

Shading done with a black felt-tipped marker, by Rudi Schermer (S). Since a marker cannot produce halftones as a pencil can, it takes a certain amount of practice to achieve good results with a marker. Even though this head has no contour lines, the observer's eye supplies them.

Two sketches done in felt-tipped marker by Christine Sauvageoll (S). These examples show how as simple an implement as a black felt-tipped marker can be used to produce very different results. The drawing on the left was done freehand in rapid shading. The one on the right was cross-hatched with the aid of a ruler.

Rubber cement 7.1

Tracing paper 3.2

Layout and visualizing paper 3.1

Another way to produce subtle tones or transitions is to dab the marker on a facial tissue, then rub the tissue over a scrap piece of paper until the tissue has dried to the point that it gives you the color tone you want. Now rub this color into your project. You will need a lot of practice with this method before you get exactly the result you want every time.

In a composition with a background and foreground (figures, objects, and so on), paint the foreground separately and paste it onto the background with rubber cement (note the section on cutting and pasting in a later section on layout and finished artwork). Because most alcohol-based markers will bleed when in contact with rubber cement, protect the surface with a special Marker Fix (Blair 10) or use a spray adhesive or wax coating. This method is easier than trying to fill in the background around objects, because that inevitably leaves visible demarcations.

Highlights and small white details do not need to be left blank. They can be added to the finished work by applying opaque white with a brush.

Visualizing (or layout) and tracing papers bring out the greatest brilliance in markers. These papers are popular for sketching and layouts because they are translucent. The preliminary sketch can simply be shoved under a sheet of such paper, which lets line drawings and lettering show through with great precision, even though visualizing and layout paper seems to be opaque. For photographs, however, tracing paper is better because it is more translucent. If the marker bleeds through the paper (make a try first), put a sheet of clear acetate between the tracing paper and the photograph to protect the photo. Color can be applied without having to do any drawing or erasing on the top sheet of paper. If contour lines are needed, they can be added after coloring.

The high transparency of these papers is a great aid in revising drawings. You can lay a first sketch under a

Four conversion variations by Elke Israng (S). Above left: Regular dot screen done with colored felt-tipped markers. Above right: Line screens and a single color area. Below: Conversions to color fields (color separation).

Sie war von englischer Kühle, italienischer Eleganz, schwedischer Blondheit und sprach
zauberhaft flämisch, und nichts als das. Meine Absichten waren überaus ernst, und so
erklärte ich mich mit etwas Sekt. Auserlesen. Trocken. Und ganz schön prickelnd. Irgendwie
scheint sie zu verstehen – aber die Absichten lustiger zu nehmen.

MM – DER SEKT MIT DEM GEWISSEN EXTRA.   PRICKELND TROCKEN.

82

Sie ist nicht Veronika, sondern Veruschka. Dies ist nicht der Empfang des Konsuls,
sondern die Party von irgend jemand. Und das ist auch kein Sekt, wie ich ihn kenne.
Sondern einer, so außergewöhnlich trocken wie ungewöhnlich prickelnd.
Kläre ich das Versehen? Oder genieße ich es weiterhin?

MM – DER SEKT MIT DEM GEWISSEN EXTRA. PRICKELND TROCKEN.

MM

EXTRA
TROCKEN
MATHEUS MÜLLER ELTVILLE · RH.
DEUTSCHER SEKT

Magazine ads done by the Leo Burnett Agency.
A layout done with colored felt-tipped markers was used to make the presentation to the client and then served as the
sketch for the photographer. The obvious similarity between the sketch and the final product speaks for itself.
Layout in felt-tipped markers: G. and J. Tillmann. Art Direction: Täuber and Täuber, Leo Burnett Agency.

Airplane drawn on visualizing paper with felt-tipped markers, by Gregor Krisztian. The plane and the background were painted separately. Then the cut-out plane was pasted onto the background.

sheet of visualizing paper and make corrections on it. If this second version is still not satisfactory, you can put it under a new sheet of visualizing paper and make still further corrections. This can go on indefinitely until you have a version that fully satisfies you.

These types of paper also make it possible to soften the intensity of some colors by applying them to the *reverse* side of the paper. In portraits, for example, you can put in the shading on the front side and then turn the paper over and put in the facial color as a single area. This prevents the fresh color from dissolving the shading and mixing with it, which could happen if the large color surface were applied to the front of the paper.

Felt-tipped marker illustration by Tom Hamilton. The locomotive was drawn on an absorbent paper so that the colors could run together and form flowing transitions.

Colored Pencils

Colored pencils 2.0

Colored leads 2.1

Colored pencils can be had in the traditional form or as mechanical pencils with appropriate leads. Colored pencils differ from regular pencils in not having degrees of hardness. However, there are 2 hard kinds: Col-Erase by Faber-Castell and Castell's TK Color leads. All other brands are more or less soft. Subtle details can be drawn with the hard pencils, which can be sharpened to a finer point. Colored pencils can be used for drawing, blending, and shading. The techniques used with regular pencils also apply here. Many colored pencils can also be painted over with water. Since they are water soluble, there is a watercolor effect afterwards.

Procedure

Building up color in a colored pencil drawing is done as follows. Begin by applying the lightest colors. Do not put heavy pressure on the pencil. Areas that will be dark in the finished drawing can be blocked in lightly now, too, but it is crucial at this early stage not to make your work too dark because it is almost impossible to erase dark shades effectively.

Repeat the application of a given color until you have achieved the deepest intensity you want. This may take as many as 20 layers of strokes. Contrasts in shading contribute immensely to the overall effect of the picture.

A drawing will be more appealing if surfaces and shadings consist of several colors. In a green area, for example, you can apply a layer of light green, one of medium green, one of light blue, and even one of brown

Colored pencils are excellent for representing
sheens in textiles. This example is by Werner
Steuer (S).

or yellow. Skin tones can be built up using turquoise green, light brown, and pink.

To produce colors of the greatest intensity, use hard, smooth drawing papers, such as high finished Bristol boards (1 to 4 ply) as well as layout and visualizing papers.

Bond paper 3.3
Layout and visualizing paper 3.1

The rougher the paper, the more visible the pores in it are. This gives a drawing an uneven quality, and if this unevenness is undesirable, it can be eliminated by filling in the pores in the paper with a sharply pointed pencil. Another way to do this is to apply watercolors first, then go over these areas with a colored pencil of the same shade. This method is useful for large areas and particularly for dark ones. The watercolor underpainting produces a more uniform color because no white is left to show through. The watercolor can be somewhat lighter than the pencil or only similar to it; the colored pencil then takes on the function of shading.

Colored-pencil drawing from a geophysical series by Richard Hartwell.

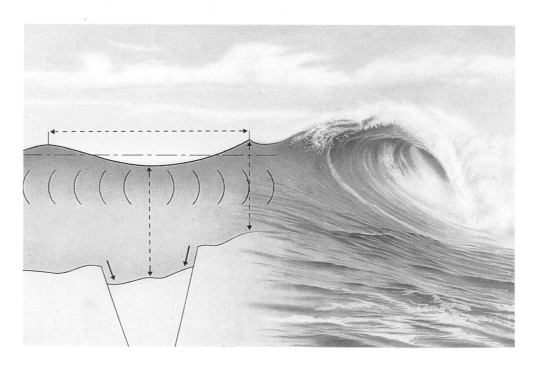

88

If watercolors will be used on a large part of the drawing, the paper should be stretched flat to prevent wrinkles from forming. This need not be done, of course, if you are working on heavy board. It is a good idea, too, to make sure in advance that the paper you want to use will take watercolors well.

Colored pencils are ideal for trips because they take up little room in your luggage and are easy to use. However, a good sharpener is an essential accessory.

Colored-pencil drawing for a postage stamp envelope by Michael Keller.

Pencil sharpener 1.3

Detail from a felt-tipped marker drawing by Claus Weidmüller. This illustration comes from a picture book (done as one of the artist's degree requirements). It was drawn on rough, cold-press illustration board with Prismacolor pencils.

Colored-pencil drawing by Chi-Ming Kan (S).

Pastels

Pastel color sticks 2.2

Pastels are colors that come in solid form as round or square sticks. These sticks break very easily, but this isn't a problem because the small pieces are handy to work with. (Note that Eberhard Faber offers a somewhat hard pastel under the name Nupastel Color Sticks.) With pastels, you can do line drawing and also fill in large areas with color; since the colors are very intense and opaque, remarkable effects can be achieved

Watercolor paper 4.2

with them, especially on handmade watercolor papers. Using blending stumps, you can produce subtle transitions by lightly rubbing over the color. The points of the

Blending stumps 1.29

blending stumps make it possible to do very precise work.

With a thin erasing template made of tin you can erase away *erasable* pastels to a sharply defined edge. Pastels are almost like a dust on the surface of the paper and can be smudged very easily. For this reason, pastel

Fixative 2.25

drawings should be treated with a fixative, but use the fixative sparingly because, unfortunately, it will dull the brilliance of the colors. American industrial designers have developed a method—called *rendering*—for making 2-dimensional representations of products. They use pastel colors and solvents and, sometimes, felt-tipped markers in the process. It is used primarily in the automobile industry for presenting new ideas in vivid form before models are built.

The Rendering Process

Layout and visualizing paper 3.4

Place your preliminary sketch under visualizing or layout paper and trace over it with a hard pencil. For the

Frisket 5.5

large parts, cut out acetate templates or friskfilm (see

the section on making templates in the later section on some techniques) and tape the first template where it belongs on the drawing. With a knife, scrape some powder off a pastel stick and mix the powder with a few drops of solvent (such as marker fluid, lighter fluid, or dry cleaning fluid). Then rub this mixture over the template with a paper towel or wad of cotton. This applies the color to the paper in a very fine layer, and depending on how you rub the color on, you can make extremely fine progressions of shading. Once the solvent has dried, colors applied this way are nowhere near as

Howard Kanovitz, "Two on Green," 1976. Pastels on shaded paper, 21″ x 28″ (53.5 x 71 cm).

93

Rendering of a pencil sharpener, done with pastels, solvent, and felt-tipped markers by Bruning on a special visualizing paper. Black marker was applied to the reverse side of the paper and appears as gray shadow on the front side. The highlights were added with opaque white.

Chalk and charcoal stick 2.4

Colored pencils 2.0

likely to smudge as pastels applied dry. Because the solvent carries the color right into the pores of the paper, pastels applied this way cannot be easily erased. But highlights can be produced by erasing either freehand or with an erasing template.

If you want to build up a shading out of several colors, rub the base color into the template, fix it, and then add the first shading with the next darker color. After fixing this partial coloration, rub on the next color. This process can be repeated indefinitely until you achieve the desired effect.

Now, remove the template and draw in the fine details, like lines, bright areas, small shadows, and so

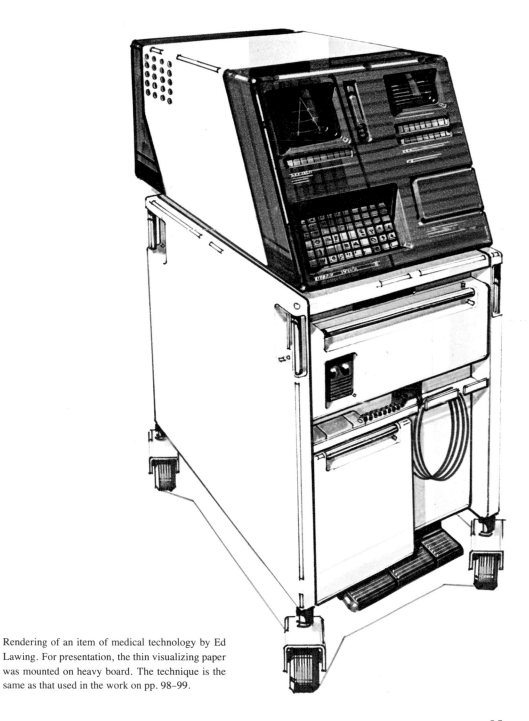

Rendering of an item of medical technology by Ed Lawing. For presentation, the thin visualizing paper was mounted on heavy board. The technique is the same as that used in the work on pp. 98–99.

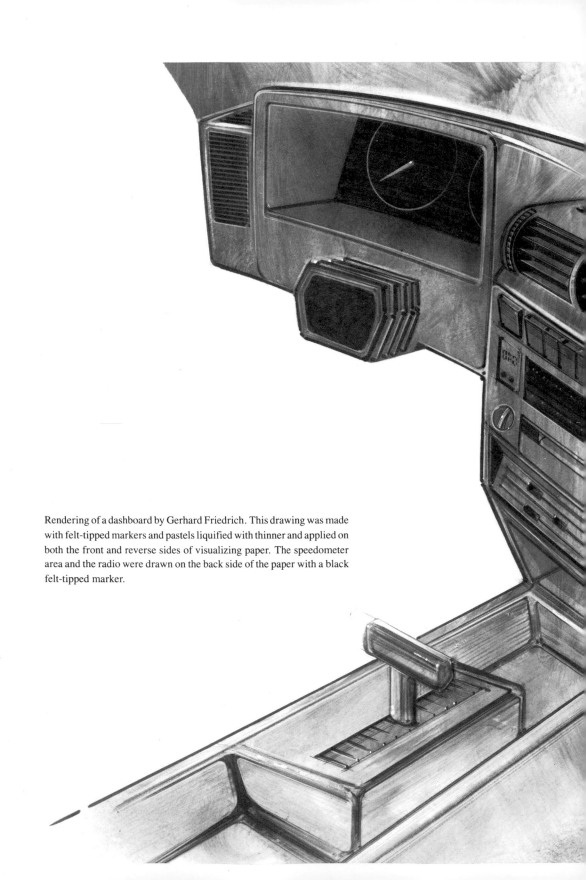

Rendering of a dashboard by Gerhard Friedrich. This drawing was made with felt-tipped markers and pastels liquified with thinner and applied on both the front and reverse sides of visualizing paper. The speedometer area and the radio were drawn on the back side of the paper with a black felt-tipped marker.

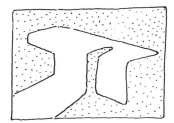

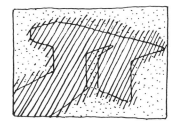

forth, with Nupastel Color Sticks or Colored Pencils, both of which can be sharpened to a finer point than pastels. Use opaque paints to add highlights or very bright areas.

If you want to place an object on a colored background, tape a template with the form of the object cut out of it over your visualizing paper and rub the liquified pastel over the template. Depending on whether you want a smooth or a textured background, you can use a paper towel, a sponge, a bristle brush, or a stipple brush to apply the still liquid color. The object can also be colored with powdered pastel alone—that is, without mixing it with solvent—by rubbing the pastel powder into the stencil with a cotton pad and then fixing the color.

Technical presentations of this kind are often done with a combination of pastel sticks, colored pencils, and felt-tipped markers. The markers most often used are Design Art Markers and Magic Markers (cool or warm gray 1 to 9). Automobile manufacturers use a paper that was developed especially to be worked on with felt-tipped markers on *both* sides. This is the vellum produced by J. Lewis Art Supply in Detroit. Shading sometimes is applied to the *reverse* side of the paper with black or dark markers. The color is diffused by the whitish paper, and the shading thus appears more fluid.

Almost all automobile renderings are done on a *very large scale* and then shot down. This allows the artist to work with a free hand because small imperfections disappear when the rendering is reduced. This technique produces very striking effects.

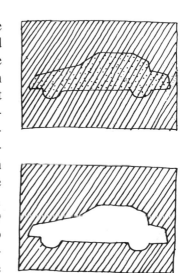

Rendering of an automobile by Gerhard Friedrich. Felt-tipped markers and pastels liquified with thinner on visualizing paper.

Rendering of a recreational vehicle by Till Altmann and Willy Ras (S). Felt-tipped markers and pastels liquified with thinner on visualizing paper (project submitted as a degree requirement). ▷

Left: Watercolor by Maria Kohl (S). Liquid watercolors on rough paper. The light areas were wiped out with paper towel while the paint was still wet.

Right: A quick watercolor sketch by Petra Hofmann (S). Liquid watercolors on rough paper.

102

Watercolors

Dry Watercolors

Watercolors in dry form are commercially available as little chips that can be bought separately or in sets. The pigments, some of which are of organic origin, are pulverized into a very fine powder, then pressed into chips; this process is what makes these colors so expensive. The range of colors available is vast, including over 100 shades.

Watercolor 2.6

The chips are moistened with water to form a solid-particulate material in suspension. Depending on how much they are thinned, they can be applied as *opaque* or highly *transparent* colors. If you use only a little water in your brush and apply a thick mixture, you will get an opaque color comparable to that achieved with an opaque watercolor. However, because dry watercolors are so expensive, this procedure is practical only for covering small surfaces.

Dry watercolors are also available in small tubes. These colors, too, are mixed with water, and once they are dry they can—at least to some extent—be dissolved again with water.

Liquid-Soluble Watercolors

Liquid watercolors come in small bottles and are a dye material in solution, sometimes referred to as dye aniline or liquid-soluble watercolors. Because these watercolors are highly concentrated, very small amounts yield satisfactory results even when heavily diluted. Some manufacturers supply droppers with each bottle. Droppers simplify measuring out precise quantities and preclude the possibility of ruining a whole bottle by dip-

Liquid aniline watercolors 2.19

ping a dirty brush into it. A single drop of liquid-soluble watercolor, diluted with water, is often enough to color an entire background.

The 2 paintings shown on page 102 were done with the 3 base colors closest to what are called *process colors* in printing—yellow, magenta (red), and cyan (blue). They show that it is not necessary to buy a complete set of watercolors. However, if you will be doing a lot of professional work, it will save you time if you own a complete set.

One disadvantage of these colors is their sensitivity to light. If a reproduction is to be made from a watercolor work, then this disadvantage is of no consequence. However, you should avoid exposing liquid-soluble watercolor originals to light for long periods of time.

Dr. Martin's Color Remover 2.20

Liquid-soluble watercolors are water soluble again after they have dried, and they can even be bleached out with a color remover or chlorine bleach. However, some colors are harder to remove than others, and not all of them can be removed entirely. It therefore pays to make tests on scrap paper. Use an old brush to do the bleaching, and blot away any excess color remover with a paper towel. Repeat the procedure until the bleach ceases to have any effect. You can repaint bleached areas immediately without fear that the newly applied color will be bleached. Bleach is very handy for making corrections, as in cases where you have accidentally painted outside a contour line.

A tip: If you have used remover and then applied a new color and you store your work in a moist area, the dampness can reactivate the chlorine bleach and therefore bleach out your new color. Consequently, watercolors that have been treated with remover should always be stored in dry rooms.

You will be interested to know that Dr. Martin's watercolors can be put into *empty* felt-tipped markers, thus enabling you both to *draw* and to paint with the same color. You can also use Dr. Martin's technical pens for fine line work.

The charm of watercolors is derived from the brilliant transparency of their soft tones and the power of their heavy ones. If layer after layer of highly diluted and therefore highly transparent watercolors are applied, they take on increasingly rich tones and impart a sense of 3-dimensionality. Remember that the structure of the painted surface, whether paper or board, shows through, and pencil and ink lines remain visible.

Apply layer upon layer of your light colors first. In this way, you can make those tones more intense or as dark as you wish. Apply the dark colors only at the end of your work (except in those areas where you know in advance that you want dark colors), because dark areas cannot always be washed out or brightened at will.

Procedures

You should keep the following points in mind when working with watercolors:

1. Choose the correct paper and stretch it if necessary.
2. Have plenty of water on hand.
3. Colors for large areas should be premixed in sufficient quantities.
4. Choose the proper brushes.
5. Transfer the preliminary drawing to your working paper.
6. If necessary, cover areas not to be colored.
7. Build up the background and remove the rubber cement.
8. Fill in the details.

Choosing the Right Paper and Stretching It
Good watercolor paper should be absorbent, but it should not let the color spread so readily that sharp contours are no longer possible. This is often the case with cheap pads. Smooth papers or boards will often not

Watercolor papers and boards 4.1 and 4.2

Watercolor boards 4.1

accept the color, will produce ugly edges later, or will make every brushstroke show. (However, there is a smooth watercolor paper that is absorbent but does not have a textured surface. This paper is, of course, excellent for watercolor work.) Of course, the coarser the texture of a watercolor paper, the easier it is to build up progressions of shading.

Watercolor paper is available in 4 forms: in single sheets, in pads, in blocks, and on boards. The last is a sheet of watercolor paper glued to a heavy cardboard.

As everyone knows from experience, paper that comes in contact with water will form wrinkles that remain after the paper dries. However, paper especially developed for watercolors will wrinkle when the paint is applied but will flatten out again completely as it dries. Therefore, the paper should be stretched *before* you begin work.

The glue that runs completely around the edges of watercolor blocks makes stretching unnecessary, and once the sheets are *completely* dry, they will also be flat again.

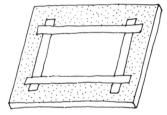

With watercolor board, the gluing together of the layers prevents wrinkling (just as the layering of plywood prevents it from warping). Still, if you will be using a lot of water, it is a good idea to mount a board on a working surface with masking tape.

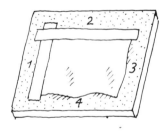

There are 3 methods for stretching watercolor paper. For 2 of them, you will need plywood or masonite boards that are large enough to leave about a 4″ (10-cm) margin around your paper.

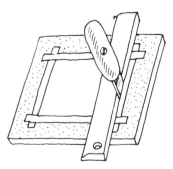

1. Attach the dry watercolor paper to your board with 4 strips of masking tape. The tape should be broad enough to keep the paper from pulling loose as you paint on it. Now you're ready to begin.
2. Dampen the reverse side of the paper with a sponge. This will make the paper expand and wrinkle. Now quickly turn it over and fasten the edges of the paper to

the board with brown packing tape, the kind that has to be moistened before it is applied. After a few tries, you will be able to master this somewhat tricky process. Do not let the wrinkles in the paper disturb you; once the paper is dry it will be stretched as tight as a drum.

3. Using rubber cement, spray adhesive, or double-sided tape, glue a sheet of watercolor paper to a sturdy piece of cardboard. This will give you a working surface as stable as that of a watercolor board. (For a description of this mounting process, see the section on layouts and finished artwork.)

Paper stretched by methods 1 and 2 will wrinkle time and again as you work with it, but when dry, it will be completely flat. After you've completed your painting, cut out the finished watercolor, using a knife and ruler, but be sure the steel inset of the cutting ruler is facing *outward* and the knife is on the outside of the ruler so that you will not accidentally cut into your work.

Water
A large container with fresh water is absolutely essential for watercolor work. You'll need the water to thin the paints and clean your brushes, and it has to be changed often. Because watercolors, even if heavily diluted, will still yield some color, it is obvious that using dirty water will dull your work. The plastic bottles that mineral water or soda come in are ideal containers for water. With scissors or a knife, cut off the conical top of the bottle, and on opposite sides of the rim, cut 2 small indentations in which to lay your brush. These notches are also handy for squeezing excess paint out of your brushes, especially if you are working with acrylics.

Canning jars can also be used as water containers. However, be aware that the special jars with separate compartments available in art supply shops are a waste of money. They are both impractical and too small.

Premixed Colors

For the larger areas in your work, you should have adequate amounts of premixed colors on hand. It is better to mix somewhat more than you expect to use rather than run the risk of not having enough, for in the watercolor techniques that call for speed, you will not have time to mix more paint while you work. Cups, porcelain palettes, and so on can be used for mixing.

Brushes

The size of the brush should be appropriate to the size of the area you want to paint. For large areas, use a flat brush or a thick round brush. For all other work, I have found a size 7 round brush very versatile. With it, you can paint in tiny areas as well as ones that are not excessively large. These brushes are expensive, but they retain their points, and that is very important. If you use them for watercolors only, they will stand up to years of use. Inexpensive watercolor brushes can be very inadequate for any exacting work.

When buying brushes, look for hairs that form a fine point and do not stick out, for you cannot do fine work with a brush that splays. You can test the quality of the bristles by wetting the brush in a glass of water, then pressing the water out by drawing the brush across the back of your hand, rotating the brush at the same time. A good brush will form a sharp point.

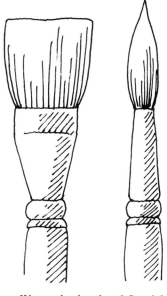

Watercolor brushes 6.0 and 6.1

The Preliminary Drawing

Very few people are so talented that they can apply watercolors directly to paper without the aid of a preliminary drawing. You can make your drawing directly on the watercolor paper, but this is not a good method if you have to do a lot of erasing, because watercolor paper tears very easily. The alternative is to make a tracing that you then transfer on to your watercolor paper with graphite paper. Draw over the graphite lines with pencil or pen and ink, lightly erase the graphite, then apply your watercolors.

Watercolor papers 4.1

Tracing paper 3.2

Graphite paper 8.0

Covering Areas to Be Left Blank

Since highly diluted watercolors are not opaque, you cannot, for example, paint a yellow area in over a blue background. However, there are 3 ways that you can produce a yellow area in a blue field:

1. Paint the dark color in around the light one.
2. Paint opaque white over the dark blue, and then put yellow over the white.
3. Cover the area that will be yellow with rubber cement.

Rubber cement 7.1

Here's a way to do the last procedure. Apply rubber cement with an old or cheap brush to the area you want to leave free of your dark background. When the cement is dry, go over the *entire* area with the blue. The watercolor left standing on the rubber cement should be dabbed away with a paper towel once the rest of the color has been absorbed into the paper. When the paper is *completely* dry, take the rubber cement away with a pick-up. If some of the blue has penetrated into the covered area, remove it with water or bleach. Now you can paint the blank area with yellow. Because rubber cement is diluted with benzol and not water, it can also be applied over watercolors without affecting them.

Building up a Background

In painting large surfaces with watercolors , it is important to work from top to bottom. For this reason, the working surface should be set at an angle of about 15° to 30° from the horizontal. Adjustable drawing boards equipped with devices that let you set them at any angle are ideal for this. The angled surface encourages a smooth flow of color and prevents the color from running back on to already painted parts of your work, which can easily happen if you apply watercolors on a horizontal surface. The steeper the angle of the board is, the faster the watercolor could form a drip, which will run down the paper, leaving a trace of color that has the fatal tendency of showing up afterwards. If you are a beginner, start with a 15° angle for your board.

The area not to be painted is covered with rubber cement. When the cement is dry, the watercolor can be quickly applied to the entire page.

The application of 2 opposing progressions: ▷
1.   Red progression.
2.   Blue progression, applied over the red progression but with the page turned 180°.

Painting around a blocked-out area:
1.   In this example, the application of the watercolor begins in the upper left-hand corner. Note that ample watercolor has been left at the hand and the head.
2.   The paint at the head is picked up with a freshly filled brush and quickly drawn downward. Once again, sufficient paint is left at the stopping point.
3.   The same process is repeated on the left side; when the bottom is reached, the 2 sides come together and the bottom is filled in, as are the 2 enclosed fields formed by the figure's legs and by her arm, torso, and skirt.
4.   Now the details that go inside the contour lines of the figure can be added.

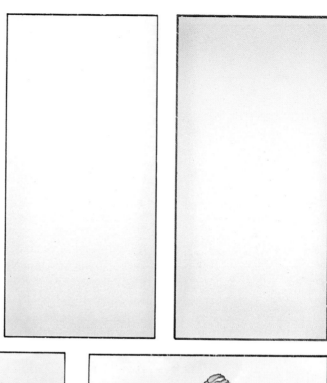

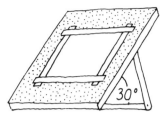

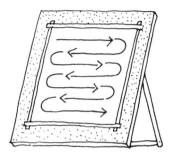

Uniform Background Once you have mounted your stretched paper onto the drawing board and mixed a sufficient amount of paint in a glass or an aluminum cup, slightly wet the paper to guarantee a perfect gradation. This can be done by using distilled water in a very soft sponge, but the sponge ought not be too wet since the watercolor paper should not be soaked, but just receive a small bit of dampness. Since the surfaces of the papers vary—some are more rugged than others—strike very lighthandedly over the paper to avoid tearing the surface.

Another possibility is to spray water on the paper with an airbrush or a spray bottle (one commonly used for moistening plants). This procedure always leaves the paper surface unharmed. allow the water to dry just a little bit—a few seconds; the surface should not look wet.

Once the paper is wet, start immediately with your color work. For larger areas, flat sable brushes (Grumbacher Aquarelle 6142) or oval camel's hair brushes (Grumbacher 55 Wash Brushes) are the best. They are fairly expensive, but if used only for watercolors and if cleaned properly, they will last forever. Take a brush filled with watercolor and, beginning in the upper left-hand corner, stroke across the paper from left to right. Then, slightly overlapping the first stroke, go back across the paper from right to left and proceed on down the paper in this zig-zag fashion without lifting your brush. When the brush is almost empty, refill so you can work quickly. The watercolor running down the paper will gather at the lower edge. Pick it up with a dry brush and wipe the brush clean on a paper towel. Be sure to remove this excess paint completely; otherwise it will be drawn into the paper by capillary action and form an undesirable border.

Shaded Background If you want a background that becomes progressively lighter from top to bottom, mix the color which will be the strongest (or darkest). Use an aluminum cup (such as one with a 2½" [5-cm] diameter and a 2" [4-cm] depth) and mix enough to fill the cup about ½" (1½ cm). Dampen your mounted paper with clean water and set jar of clean water aside. Make your first brushstrokes as described for a uniform background, but before you fill the nearly empty brush again, dip it briefly in the clean water and then stir the brush in your color cup so that the color will be diluted. Now apply your next strokes, dip the brush in water again, thinning the color still more, and proceed in this fashion down to the bottom of the paper. It is especially important to remove the liquid that gathers at the bottom, because otherwise a dark edge will form on what should be the lightest area of the painting.

Brushes 6.0 and 6.1

Do not expect instant success with your first attempts at shading with watercolor. This technique requires some practice, particularly because the surface will look quite perfect while still wet, but may reveal stripes and mistakes vividly when dry. It is important, too, to work quickly and not to go back over dry or drying sections with a wet brush to make corrections. Doing this will inevitably produce clouds or strips.

If you want shading from light at the top to dark at the bottom, use the procedure just described and simply turn your paper upside down. Or if you already have a preliminary drawing on the paper, turn it on its head and apply the shading in this position.

Note, of course, that you can add your preliminary drawing after the background has been painted in.

Backgrounds with Opposing Shadings Sometimes you will want to portray images for a poster or a film animation that require opposing progressions of shading, such as skies or colored backgrounds. For example, see the illustration on page 110, which uses a red-blue combination. To accomplish this, paint a shading, beginning with a highly diluted scarlet lake. By the time you reach the bottom, by constantly diluting your color, the last few strokes will leave only the faintest hint of

Magazine illustration (a reduced detail) by Tom Hamilton. Liquid watercolor on heavy watercolor paper. In this kind of wet-on-wet painting, the colors run into each other.

Watercolor with 2 opposing progressions as the background. All the other parts of the picture are painted in the same colors but in greater concentrations. Liquid watercolor on rough paper (reduction).

stration by Roberto Innocenti from a book on the Russo-Japanese war. Watercolors on heavy watercolor paper. This detail shows the
eptionally fine pen lines that enclose all the fields of color. The lines also are done with pen and watercolor.

pink on the paper. Let the paper dry until it is completely flat again. Now turn the paper upside down and paint a shading beginning with medium-strength Winsor blue and ending with a very light shade of blue.

Special Techniques

There is one problem in painting backgrounds (skies, structured or textured parts such as walls, rocks, etc.) which consist of 2 or more layers of color. Since the second layer to some degree dissolves the first one, the colors blend where not desired or the textures are dissolved and disappear entirely. This happens more often when the consistency of the watercolor is thicker—that is, not very diluted. To avoid this to some degree, use one of 2 techniques.

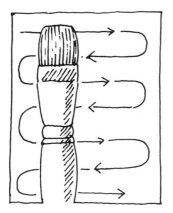

Washing Out Washing out is a way to lighten, soften, or partially remove color already applied to a surface. After you have painted a uniform or shaded background, let the paper dry. Place the piece on the inclined drawing board and start washing down the paper from top to bottom, using a bristle brush and clear water in zig-zag strokes.

By the time you reach the bottom, the color layer is very light. Let the paper dry, and turn it upside down if you want opposing shadings and apply the second layer. Let the second layer dry and repeat the washing procedure. You can superimpose as many layers as you want, as the color "bites" into the paper. You achieve some very delicate and beautiful backgrounds or skies with this manifold layering, since the transparency of the washed-out colors creates a magic depth.

For washing out, use a top-quality watercolor paper, such as the handmade papers (see 4.2), because the repeated strokes of the bristle brush might hurt the surface. Instead of a bristle brush, you could use a soft sponge but even that might harm the paper. If the paper is damaged, the color you use to fill in details will overflow the border lines. You can't control it, and can't see the damage as it occurs. It pays to make tests in advance with several papers.

This procedure of repeated shadings, washing, and dryings requires—as you can well imagine—a great deal of time. It is worthwhile only if you do several pieces at once and store them. Get a number of plywood or Masonite boards, stretch watercolor paper on them, and paint 5 or 10 backgrounds in one session.

Texturing   To achieve a textured effect, you can use sponges (fine and coarse), cloth, paper towels, crumbled paper, or any of several other textured items. Soak with the color and press it to the paper to create the desired effect. If you make the textures as your first layer and then follow with a wash, the wash will dissolve the textured effects. Of course, you can make the texturing your last layer, but there is another way. Just add some drops of casein (which is waterproof after drying) to your watercolor, texture as you wish, and let it dry. The textured layer is now waterproof and you can layer it with a normal wash or with new textures in another watercolor-casein combination. This method also opens up innumerable possibilities for experimentation.

Adding Details
Now that you have learned how to begin a watercolor painting, it is time to pay attention to the details of your compositions. Add all figures and objects in as great or as little complexity as you wish, depending on the effect you wish to achieve. You may want to combine techniques or media in your work (see the section on some mixed techniques at the end of the next section).

To preserve the chromatic unity of a picture, such as a landscape, paint the details, such as mountains, trees, houses, people, animals, and so on, using the *same* colors you used in the sky, only in more or less intense dilutions. Always begin with pale dilutions. When the

come and see

An ad by Günter Blum. Liquid watercolor on board. The draft was about 3 times larger than the printed ad.
The colors were built up layer upon layer. The light areas were scraped out with a razor blade.

Illustration from the book *By Camel or by Car* by Guy Billout. Ink and watercolor on watercolor paper. The watercolor was applied over the blue ink drawing with airbrush and brush.

color is dry, you can always add more color if you need it. This method of layering makes it easier to control the chromatic structure of the picture. As an aid to remembering the colors used—and this applies particularly to backgrounds prepared in advance—write on the margin or the back of the picture the colors you used, perhaps noting their numbers as well. If you do lose track of the colors you have used, it is often very difficult to reconstruct them.

Painting Around an Area

In some cases you will be obliged to paint around a given area without being able, or wanting, to cover it. As a rule, edges of drying color will form where you stop painting to refill your brush. These edges can be avoided with the following method: With your work on an angled drawing board, start on the left side and paint in toward the area to be left blank. When you reach the contour line, stop and leave a drop of color standing on the paper, but not so much that it drips down. Now proceed to the other side of the blank area and paint in from the right side to the same level, leaving a drop of color here, too. Fill your brush and pick up the drop on the left and paint down the page. Repeat this process, moving from left to right, until you have fully enclosed the area in question.

Drawing board 1.20

The important thing to watch is that the drop of color on the side where you are not working does not dry out. If it does and an edge of color forms, try to dissolve it carefully with a brush only slightly dampened with water. Go back and forth over the area with zig-zag motions, then soak up the excess color with a paper towel. The procedure described here should be carried out very quickly so that dry spots cannot form.

Painting Wet on Wet

Wet-on-wet painting is a popular technique that offers a rich field for experimentation. In this procedure, a dif-

120

ferent color is dabbed in, or painted over, a color that is still wet. The new color spreads out in the one already on the paper and forms so-called clouds. This technique is not so easy to control unless you have experience with it, but it produces such striking structures and color combinations that every graphic artist should learn to use it.

It also offers a way to create shadings. To make them in small areas, dab away the still-wet color with a paper towel. Depending on your degree of skill, this can produce transitions from pale tones to full ones. Areas already painted in can be moistened again with a brush and water, and clouds can then be dabbed into these damp areas.

Photo Ace

When used with liquid-soluble watercolors, Photo Ace will "adhere" or "bite into" the photo surface emulsion. Although it is not water resistant when it is dry, it can be made so with a special fixative. Too heavy applications can also be lightened with bleach.

Photo Ace 2.22

Using Photo Ace

This color can be applied with cotton, a brush, or an airbrush. With cotton dipped in acetone (available in drugstores), wipe the surface of the photographic paper to clean off any traces of grease or fingerprints. Mix the color in a saucer in a *much thinner mixture* than the tone you want. Before applying the color, wipe the paper with cotton dipped in water so that the gelatin will swell up a little. When the water has penetrated into the layer and while it is still damp, apply the first layer of color in even strokes with a cotton wad. The proper color tone is

Illustration by Dieter Ziegenfeuter. Photo Ace and liquid watercolor applied to a photograph with brush and cotton.

achieved by repeated applications. Otherwise, if you were to mix the color in the concentration you desired, you would produce clouds that either could not be removed at all or could be only partially removed with a bleaching agent.

If you want to block off certain areas when you are painting or spraying, you can cover them with frisket. Apply this film with a cheap brush. When it dries, you can begin painting or spraying over it. When you are done, you can then peel the film off whole once you have started a corner of it with a knife. This frisket film *cannot* be used on papers or boards with rough surfaces because it penetrates into the pores and then cannot be completely removed.

Frisket 5.5

In an airbursh, liquid aniline watercolor is used like a thinned watercolor. Keep the pressure low, and do not spray too heavily. Rather, let the work dry, then repeat applications until you have the color intensity you want.

Colored Inks

Colored inks, also known as India or drawing inks, are sold in jars and bottles. After drying, these inks become waterproof and cannot be dissolved anymore. For this reason, they are a popular medium for underpainting. You can use watercolors or tempera over drawing-ink underpainting and then wash them off again without damaging the underpainting below. Unlike liquid watercolors, drawing inks should be thinned only with distilled or boiled water.

Waterproof colored drawing inks 2.23

Watercolors 2.6 and 2.19
Tempera 2.9

The one great advantage drawing ink has is that it is waterproof. Apart from this, liquid watercolors are much easier to use and more versatile. Drawing ink is used primarily for pen-and-ink drawing. The sepia shade is a very popular one for this purpose.

It's interesting to note that Charlie White III, one of the most famous American airbrush artists, has taken to using Pelikan drawing inks in his airbrush because they are much more resistant to light than liquid watercolors.

Opaque Paints

Whereas an error in watercolors is either very difficult or impossible to correct, the opaque quality of gouache, tempera, casein, acrylics, and resin-base paints allows the artist to cover over an area repeatedly and so correct previous errors.

Layering

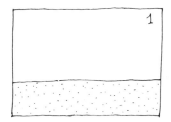

In a landscape, the sky is painted in first with a flat bristle brush, and the horizontal strokes run beyond the area that will be filled with sky in the final painting. Now, over the lower part of the sky, paint in the ground in thin layers (which may crisscross each other) until the color covers the entire area. The next largest areas of the preliminary drawing are now traced onto the work and colored in. Then come the next smaller units, and so on. The painting is thus constructed like a many-layered sandwich. The highlights, the shading, and the finest details are painted in that order. Thus, with a tree, you paint the trunk and the branches first and then the leaves.

Shadings/Transitions

Progressions of shadings cannot be created with these quickly drying opaque paints, as you could with oils by wiping the paints into each other or, as with watercolors, by letting the colors run together. Therefore you have to resort to fine brushstrokes or dots. This will not work with large areas, of course, and all you can do is use an airbrush or, using a flat brush, blend your colors in a rapid wet-on-wet application.

Bristle brush 6.3

In shading with a brush—just as in pen-and-ink shading—shadows, highlights, and transitions are often represented by crisscrossing lines. The only difference is that here a *fine brush* is used instead of a pen. The first shading lines should be executed in a color that does not contrast sharply with the background. As additional lines are added, increase the color contrast gradually until the final (and darkest or lightest) layer is reached.

Watercolor brushes 6.0 and 6.2

Another common shading technique is a "split brush" or "dry brush" method in which the brush carries only enough moisture and color to release it in very fine parallel lines through the divided and spread tips of the individual bristles when the brush is drawn across the surface. It is especially useful for reproduction work because the line-texture holds in camera and takes $1/4$ to $1/10$ the time of the former method.

The Dot Method

With this method—called pointillism—shadows, highlights, and transitions are rendered with small dots applied to the surface with the tip of the brush. The entire painting consists of dots that either overlap or are placed next to each other. Here, all the application of the colored dots does is lend plasticity to the work. As with brush shading just described, gradations of color are used. The first layer of dots shows the least contrast with the surface, the last layer, the greatest.

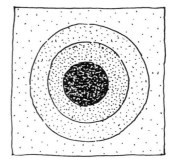

Steps in painting with opaque colors (acrylic on board):

1. First layer of brown and green on the pre-painted blue background. The paints are relatively thin.
2. Second application of brown and green. The colors still do not cover completely.
3. After the fourth application of brown and green, quite a thin yellow is applied in shading strokes with a fine retouching brush.
4. Now additional strokes of yellow are added until the desired intensity is achieved. The many thin strokes produce the opaque yellow shapes.

126

Illustration for a children's reader. Acrylic on cold-press illustration board. The reader of the book is asked to search for the animals hidden in the picture. The fields of the sky and the lake were applied with an airbrush; the trees, bushes, and grass were painted in later in a mixture of dark green and brown with retouching brushes sizes 1 to 4. The light areas were then worked up with many layers of thinned paint; the animal figures were the last things to be painted in. The vague, light stripes on the surface of the water were made by spraying through 2 rulers raised off the work. (see The Airbrush).

The light areas and the shadows were dotted in with a very fine brush on a stippled background. The dots are almost impossible to see even in the original. This detail is on a scale of 1:1, acrylic on board. Working time, about 60 hours. Term project by Volkmar Hoppe.

Two details from Alex Colville's "My Father and His Dog." Acrylic on wood. The entire painting is made up of many layers of individual colored dots that produce the background, the highlights, and the shadows. One exception is the hair, which is done with strokes.

Gouache and Tempera

Gouache 2.7
Tempera 2.9

Gouache and tempera are available in tubes and jars. These opaque colors are mixed with water and can be dissolved again with water after they have dried. Gouache is more expensive and produces more intense colors than tempera, but it can also be mixed with tempera. Gouache is available in about 80 colors, tempera in about 24 colors.

In applying these paints it is easy to yield to the temptation to cover the surface right away. But as a rule the paint will be mixed *too thick*. If you use it that way, the flat areas will have stripes in them and show high points that become shiny if you rub your hand over them often. Therefore, to get a flat and even coloration, apply the paint in a *thin* layer and in a *crisscross pattern*. Begin with a horizontal layer. Then, when this is dry, add a vertical one. Repeat this until the desired degree of opacity is reached. Both gouache and tempera are extremely susceptible to scratches and abrasions and also to water. It is therefore a good idea to coat finished work with a matte or glossy varnish applied with a varnish brush or a spray can.

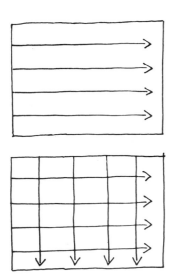

Since gouache and tempera are easy to work with—water soluble, quick drying, readily painted over, dissolvable again if they have dried on the palette—they are often used for underpainting in oil paintings (this is one of the oldest mixed techniques). Backgrounds and details are blocked in with these quick-drying paints.

Oil paint 2.15

The oil paints applied over them cannot affect them because gouache and tempera are soluble only in water.

With opaque white—a color available in tempera—you can imitate engraving or embossing (useful, for example, for a mock-up presentation). Engraving or embossing is produced by using a steel stamp on the back of a piece of paper or board; the method can be used to produce not only raised lettering but also ornaments, borders, small patterns on letter paper, and so on. Because opaque white has a lot of "body" and stands out in a layer on any surface to which it is applied, you can produce a plastic effect by carefully building up layers of it. Before applying a layer, be sure the previous one is *absolutely* dry.

Casein (Plaka)

Casein, or plaka, is a paint that is not particularly intense and not available in many shades. However, it can be mixed with gouache and tempera, and this enlarges its color range somewhat. For painting, it is thinned with water, is uncomplicated to use, and is highly opaque. It also has the great advantage of being waterproof after it dries. It can be painted over repeatedly without any danger of bleeding through. It is ideal for stippling, since a new layer doesn't dissolve the previous one, as could happen if you use tempera or gouache. Casein can also be used in airbrushes. However, airbrushes should be cleaned immediately after such use because once casein has dried, it is very difficult to remove. Palettes should be cleaned right away, too. Old plates or glass are ideal for casein because it is easy to scrape dried paint off them with a spatula.

Casein should be applied like gouache or tempera. Here, too, it pays to apply the paint in a crisscross pattern to achieve even surfaces (as described in the section on gouache and tempera). Bristle brushes are ideal for painting large surfaces; but, just like the finer brushes you use for detail work—and here I would recommend using cheap watercolor brushes—these brushes must be washed out *immediately* and *carefully,* using soap for the final washing. If this is not done, the paint will collect in the ferrule and soon spread the bristles.

Casein 2.11

Stipple brush 6.5

Airbrush 6.21

Bristle brush 6.3

131

Calendar illustration (detail on a scale of 1:1). Part of a final exam project by Karin Weber. The larger areas, like the rocks, are stippled in, then finished with a fine brush. Acrylic on board.

Book jacket by Allan Manham, done for Penguin books. Acrylics were used because of their opacity, canvas because of its texture.

Resin-Base Paints

Resin-base paint 2.12

Resin-base paints are much cheaper than casein or acrylics, and they are sold in paint stores for use in coloring wall paints. They come in plastic bottles and can be used like casein or acrylics. They, too, are waterproof after drying.

Acrylic Paints

Acrylic paint 2.13

Spatula 6.7

Airbrush 6.21

Once applied, acrylics resemble oils. They have the same sheen and the same plastic effect. They can be applied with a brush or a spatula directly out of the tube (that method is called impasto), or—*thinned with water*—they can be applied in any consistency from opaque to transparent with a brush or airbrush.

The medium in acrylic paints is a synthetic resin similar to acrylic glass. Mixed with water, acrylic paints dry almost as quickly as casein. This makes them excellent for sketching, particularly because they are waterproof after drying.

Surfaces and Grounds

Primer 2.19

Acrylics will adhere to any surface that is free of oil. Those most commonly used are paper, board, canvas, and acetate. With Gesso, a white primer, materials like wood or Masonite that have not already been treated can be primed. This process is called *preparing a ground*.

Working with the Paints

I have been most satisfied with Liquitex acrylics, which come in 12 transparent and 18 opaque shades. However, not all the opaque colors cover the surface to the same extent, and you will often have to repeat the process of painting over an area, letting it dry, and painting over again until you get the coverage you want. This process may seem like a lot of trouble at first, but you will soon get used to it and not notice the extra time it costs you.

How much you should dilute your paints depends on a number of factors. If you want a relatively smooth surface, you cannot have too thick a mix. Thick paint leaves visible brushstrokes behind as it dries. However, thin paint will cover only after repeated applications and requires more time. It is therefore advisable to mix your paint on the thin side and apply it in thin, criss-crossing layers. For building up large areas of color and for shading you can use the method described above in the section on opaque paints.

Because mixed acrylic paints are heavier in consistency than tempera or casein, a short retouching brush, such as Dick Blick's detailer or pointed brushes, is better for detailed work than a brush with long, fine bristles. For large areas, you can use the usual bristle and flat brushes. Remember, though, that brushes used with acrylic paint should be washed out immediately after use, or the paint will harden them rapidly. Synthetic fiber brushes are preferable because they do not absorb water and thereby spread the ferrule.

Retouching brush 6.2

Bristle brush 6.3

Shadings

If you have worked with oils, you will find acrylics a difficult medium. Even when applied impasto, acrylics dry so quickly that they do not permit wet-on-wet paint-

Illustration by Roy Ellsworth for an article on traditional recipes in the London *Times*. Acrylic on canvas.

ing. To use this technique, you have to add a retarder that can extend the drying process to as long as 8 hours.

Here's how to adapt the technique to acrylics. Mix both colors separately and add retarder to them. Apply the first color and brush it toward the area where the second one will be. Now apply the second color and brush it toward the first so that the 2 colors begin to mix in the middle zone. The shading results from the process of mixing the 2 colors. Finish the work off by running a fresh, dry brush over it to smooth out the shading. This is a skill that requires some practice.

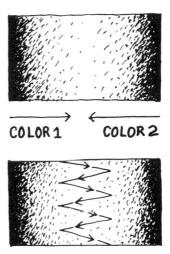

COLOR 1   COLOR 2

"The Mallard," poster by Bob Murdoch, Wurlitzer Studio; sprayed gouache on textured board.

Watercolor Effects

Acrylics can take on the character of watercolors if they are thinned with a lot of water or with a *polymer medium.* Polymer is the medium used in acrylics, and adding more of it increases the brilliance of the paint. But, unlike watercolors, acrylics cannot be dissolved or mixed on the paper again once they are dry.

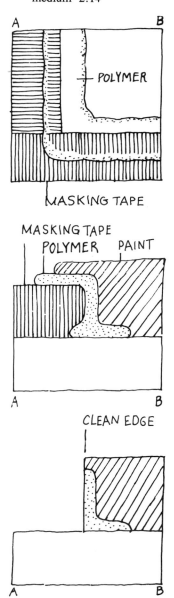

Liquitex and Aquatec Acrylic medium 2.14

Polymer Acrylic Mediums

Polymer acrylic mediums have another use apart from that of lending transparency to acrylic paints. If you want to produce a smooth border of color, you ordinarily put masking tape around the edges of your work, but what can often happen is that paint leaks under the masking tape and makes an irregular border. This can be avoided if you take a brush and run a strip of acrylic medium about ½ ″ (1 cm) wide around your work, covering the joint between the masking tape and the painting surface. The colorless medium penetrates under the masking tape and prevents any paint from leaking in. Once the medium is dry, you can then lay down your color. When it is dry, use a cutting ruler and a knife to cut carefully along the edge of the masking tape, slicing through both the paint and the medium. When you take the tape away, the edge of your work will be absolutely clean.

A matte medium will give the paints a satiny finish. If you want a shiny finish, use a glossy medium.

Using Paste

Modeling paste is used primarily to produce 3-dimensional effects on canvas or other surfaces. This paste

138

can be mixed with paint or sand and applied with a spatula. You can apply very diluted acrylics on this surface with the same layer-upon-layer technique you use for watercolors.

The Durability of Acrylic Paints

When acrylics dry, a rubberlike film forms over them and prevents water from penetrating. However, if you should drip water on a finished work, dab it off with a paper towel. Pale spots will disappear when the moisture dries.

If you spatter paint on a finished work, remove the spots *immediately* with a damp cloth. Fresh spots can be wiped away without the slightest risk to the dry paint underneath. Unlike tempera and casein, acrylic paint does not instantly penetrate the surface and mix with it.

Black-and-White Mechanicals with Mars Black (Liquitex)

Because of its durability, opacity, and ease of application with either brush or pen, black acrylic paint—Mars Black—is an excellent medium for mechanicals. It is, in any case, preferable to tempera since it is waterproof and resistant to fingerprints.

Spraying

In spraying, liquid paints or paints made liquid are driven through an airbrush by compressed air, or CO_2, and sprayed through a nozzle in a cone shape. How the

Airbrush 6.21

139

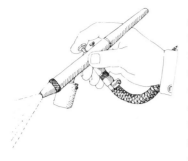

airbrush performs depends on the amount of pressure used. Low pressure (under about 30 pounds per square inch) produces a sprinkling of paint, that is, the paint comes out of the nozzle in large droplets. High pressure (over 45 pounds per square inch) produces a finer application of the paint but, at the same time, that mist is unpleasant and not particularly healthful for the artist, so always wear a mask when spraying large areas. The optimum pressure is about 37 pounds per square inch; but here, too, the option to regulate the pressure is up to you.

Most spraying is done with the aid of templates. That is, you cover part of your work with a template, and this gives the sprayed areas more or less precise contours. However, you can "paint" or "write" freehand, with an airbrush, but this requires a lot of practice.

The discussion below will be limited to those procedures that call for the use of templates.

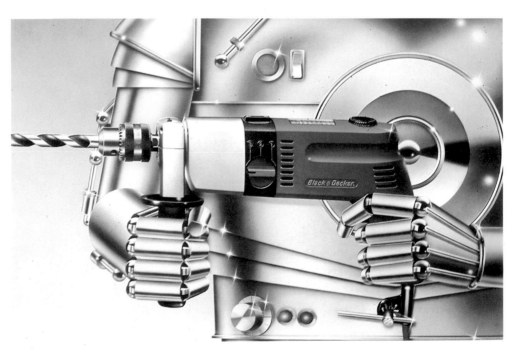

Airbrush work by Walter Pepperle for Black and Decker. Matte retouching paints on board. Some of the templates were raised off the work slightly to create blurred lines.

How the Airbrush Works

The Paasche model V-1 airbrush is designed for fine detail and for use on small areas. The paint container is open, and paint can be put into it with a dropper or a brush. The handiest all-around airbrush is the Paasche model V-2. It can be used both for fine work and for larger areas. It has the additional advantage of interchangeable paint containers. For work larger than 19″ x 24″ (48 x 61 cm) an airbrush with a still larger nozzle opening is advisable.

"Locomotive," draft for a postage stamp. Tempera sprayed over adhesive templates. The details were painted in later with fine brushes.

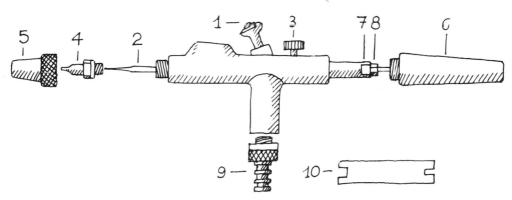

1. Lever
2. Needle
3. Thumbscrew (links the needle to the spraying mechanism)
4. Paint nozzle
5. Air jet
6. Handle cap
7. Nozzle Adjustment
8. Hexagonal nut (*never* requires adjustment)
9. Hose attachment with gasket
10. Nozzle wrench (with 3 mm and 4 mm openings)

Cleaning the Airbrush

To disassemble the airbrush for cleaning, unscrew the handle cap, loosen the thumbscrew, and remove the needle *very carefully.* Clean any paint off the needle with a paper towel and oil the needle lightly by drawing it through a cloth with a few drops of oil on it. Remove the air jet and then, with the 3 mm opening in the wrench, remove the paint nozzle. Acrylic paint is particularly likely to clog the paint nozzle with particles and make the airbrush spit. Using an old needle, or working very carefully with a new one, push the dried paint through the nozzle from behind. Do not use too much pressure, or you may damage the nozzle. Continue to clean the nozzle in this way until you can see through it when you hold it up to the light.

Manufacturers recommend rubbing candle wax into the threads of the paint nozzle to prevent paint from sticking in them. After the nozzle is screwed back in, the surplus wax can be carefully brushed away with an old toothbrush. Now tighten the nozzle lightly with the wrench but only to the point where it is firmly seated. (Be careful not to tighten the nozzle too tightly; the threads can break off very easily.) Now carefully push the needle back into the paint nozzle, seat it with light pressure, and set the thumbscrew. If you press too hard, the paint nozzle will be enlarged and can tear, or it will become funnel shaped and interfere with the shape of the spray.

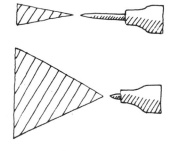

The placement of the needle influences the shape of the spray cone. If the needle extends far beyond the paint nozzle, the spray cone will be narrow. The farther back in the nozzle the needle is, the wider the cone becomes and the larger the areas are that can be sprayed with it. Before screwing the air jet back on, pull back the spray lever, which will in turn retract the needle. This prevents the needle from being damaged or bent when you replace the air jet. A bent needle makes it impossible to spray with precision.

When reassembling the brush take particular care that all the parts are screwed together snugly. Loose parts can affect the air stream adversely and so lead to unsatisfactory results. The lever controls the amounts of air and paint passing through the brush. When the lever is pulled part way back, air is released. When it is pulled back farther, the needle moves back with it. Paint should begin to flow after the lever has traveled about $1/10$ of its path. This can be adjusted by using the 4 mm opening in the nozzle wrench on the nozzle adjustment. Replace the handle cap, and the brush is ready to use.

Using the Airbrush

The steps in spraying are as follows:

1. Make a preliminary drawing and prepare your board.
2. Cut out templates.
3. Prepare your workarea.
4. Mix your paints.
5. Mount your templates and spray.
6. Wash and clean your airbrush.

Preparing the Board

For spraying, it is best to use a sturdy board that will not warp from having the paint sprayed on it. With a light pencil line, mark the borders of your work, and outside these borders, make up to 4 rows of register marks, according to your needs. Number these marks. Now lay your tracing paper on the board so that the outer borders of the tracing and the lines on the board correspond. Go over the register marks on the tracing paper with a technical pen. Now put clear masking tape around the edge of the board outside the borders of your work, so that the register marks are showing through.

Bristol board 3.4

Tracing paper 3.2

Technical pen 1.10

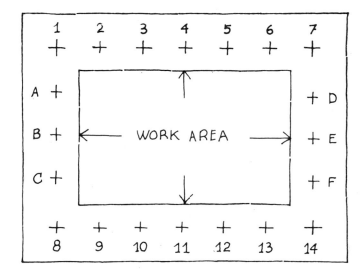

Illustration for a children's reader. The sky and the desert were sprayed onto the board in acrylic paints. The acetate templates (about .5 mm thick) used for the dunes were raised off the work about 2 mm to create soft transitions. The figures were painted in last.

Cutting Templates

A template is a cut-out form through which you can spray or stipple. While templates can be made from a number of different materials, here we'll discuss how to use 2 types: adhesive and nonadhesive.

Adhesive Templates Cut a piece of frisket material large enough to lay it with its protective paper over your preliminary drawing. Trace the shape you want, plus the register marks, with a technical pen. Now place the frisket on a soft board and cut out the form with a film cutter; for large forms, you can also use fine scissors. Since the template needs to adhere only on the edges, turn it over, raise the protective paper around the edge of the cut-out form, and cut away a border about 1/4″ to 1/2″ (1 to 2 cm) wide. Use this same method to cut away the protective paper under the register marks. Now turn the film over again and line up the register marks on the template with those on your board. Press down all around the perimeter of the form so that the template adheres to the board and no paint can leak under it during spraying.

You can also cut the masking film right on the board. Trace the shapes you want to spray directly onto the frisket, which should be *lightly* stuck to the board. Use a film cutter to cut out the form. Press hard enough to just cut through the film. Lift the form out carefully with the knife and stick it on to the protective paper. You may well have use for it later. The danger with this method is that the adhesive from the film may damage paint already on the board when the stencil is removed. Also, beginners tend to press too hard on the knife and cut into the board, leaving visible marks in the finished work.

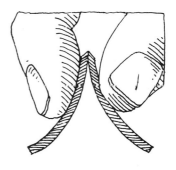

Nonadhesive Templates Nonadhesive templates are made of clear acetate between .08 and .12 mm thick. Draw the form and the register marks onto the acetate with a technical pen and then cut only lightly along the lines. Do not cut *through* it. Now pick up the acetate and

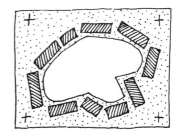

Airbrush work by Charlie White III, poster for Levi's; liquid water color on board.

Illustration by Gilda Belin; size 20″ x 28″ (50 x 70 cm). Liquid watercolors and rctouching paints were applied with an airbrush, some of them through adhesive templates and others—in the bright areas and shadows—freehand.

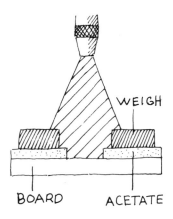

WEIGH

BOARD   ACETATE

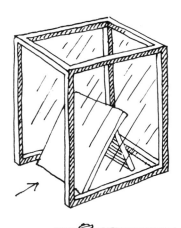

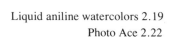

bend it along the lines you have cut into it, squeezing the joint between your thumb and forefinger until you see it break. Then lift the form out. The edges can be smoothed with sandpaper.

This kind of template has to be held down on your work with lead weights. (Slugs that printers use in typesetting are ideal for this.) Place the bars as close to the edge of the form as you can to keep the acetate from bending under the air pressure but not so close that they interfere with the spray cone. When spraying, hold the airbrush as near to vertical as possible.

Preparing the Workplace
The larger the nozzle opening, the larger the spray cone will be and the more paint particles will fly around in the air, sticking to everything. If you do not have a special room you can reserve for spraying, you can build a hood out of lath and plastic sheeting. Or you can at least hang plastic sheeting around the workarea. The plastic drop cloths sold in paint stores are ideal for this.

Install a holder on the worktable to hang your airbrush on when it's not in use. You can buy holders, but 2 nails will serve just as well.

Now I would like to pass on a tip from an airbrush expert: Paper that has been warmed takes paint better than paper at room temperature. Also, the spraying process is speeded up and is cleaner. To warm the paper evenly, you will have to build a special device that cannot be had on the market. The base of this device consists of an aluminum plate and a thermostatically regulated heating element from a heating pad.

Mixing the Paints
You can use the following paints in an airbrush.

Liquid aniline watercolors 2.19 Photo Ace 2.22	Liquid Aniline Watercolors	These do not need to be thinned for spraying.
Retouching colors 2.10	Retouching paints	This finely ground tempera was especially designed for spraying.

148

Watercolor	
Tempera	All these paints have to be thinned with
Casein	water before spraying.
Acrylics	

Gouache 2.7
Tempera 2.9
Casein 2.11
Acrylic paint 2.13

Thin the paint to the point where it can be sprayed; that is, it should just barely drip from the tip of a brush. Here, too, it pays to experiment a bit until you have found just the right proportion of paint and water. The paint has to be stirred *thoroughly* and be completely free of solid pigment (that is, unthinned lumps). It is a good idea to run acrylics and casein through a fine sieve before using them in an airbrush.

If the paint is not thin enough, either nothing will come out of the nozzle, or the airbrush will spit paint erratically. In either case, pour the paint back into its mixing container and thin it some more. The airbrush will have to be cleaned, too. After cleaning, spray clear water through it. Since some artists prefer irregular blots, done by an airbrush, the manufacturers sell a nozzle which produces such blots.

If the paint is too thin, drops will form on the work and be visible after the paint dries. Either reduce the pressure somewhat (liquid aniline watercolors form drops when used under full pressure), or thicken your paint. If you are using paints that dry very quickly, you will have to wash out the airbrush frequently. Casein tends to plug up the nozzle quickly. Under no circumstances should you let any waterproof paint dry inside the airbrush.

Mounting Templates and Spraying

If you are going to paint a number of areas with the same color that are quite far apart in your work, you can—to save acetate—cut out several templates and cover the rest of the work with cheap paper (drawing 1).

You can also cut out all the forms for the *different colors* from one piece of acetate that covers your entire

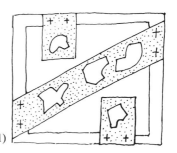

(1)

149

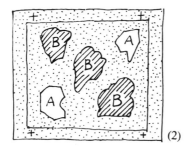

(2)

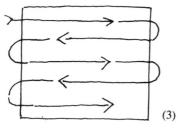

(3)

work surface. To use, first cover the forms B and spray color A. Then cover forms A and spray color B. This can be done with as many colors as you like (drawing 2).

After filling your airbrush, test it on a piece of scrap paper to be sure it is working properly. If you pull the lever back lightly, you get a weak spray. If you pull it all the way back, you get a stronger spray.

Spray large areas with a sweeping, back-and-forth motion (drawing 3). Move the airbrush at a slow but constant speed and with a *constant air pressure,* moving horizontally from left to right and back again. Be sure to go beyond the edge of your work and continue to spray as you make the turns and move back toward the other side. Continue in this fashion to the bottom of the paper. It is crucial to work continuously, briskly, and with steady movements. After the first spraying, the paint might not cover completely or be even. Repeat the spraying procedure as often as you need to get the coverage and evenness you want.

In spraying large areas, it is important to retract the needle as far as it will go to make the largest possible spray cone. By running out beyond the edges of your work and not interrupting the spray you can avoid borders or heavier concentrations of color at the turns. If you stop your motion at any point, the paint will be applied more heavily, and you probably will not notice this until you are finished. This is why you must keep the airbrush in motion *at all times.*

Shading   To spray shading, you reverse the process you use for watercolors and begin at the *bottom* of the work. Using horizontal back-and-forth motions, work from bottom to top. Just short of the upper edge, stop spraying. Go back to the bottom and repeat the process, but this time stop spraying somewhat lower than you did the first time. Repeat this process, stopping a little bit lower each time until you have the desired effect. It is important to keep track of the color gradation as you

Draft for a calendar. The basic color of the blossom was stippled in casein; the orange areas and the shadings were then added in thin casein applied with an airbrush.

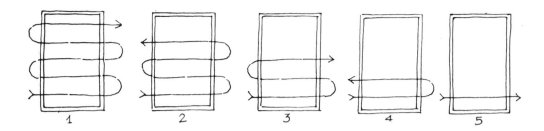

1 2 3 4 5

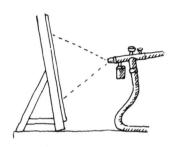

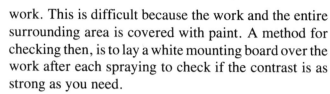

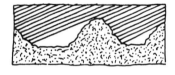

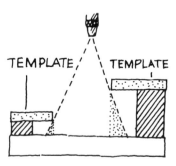

TEMPLATE   TEMPLATE

work. This is difficult because the work and the entire surrounding area is covered with paint. A method for checking then, is to lay a white mounting board over the work after each spraying to check if the contrast is as strong as you need.

The closer to *vertical* the spray cone is when it hits the paper, the flatter and more even the shading will look. To ensure that no puddles form on the board, let it dry after each thin application of paint. Then go ahead to add another and another until you have the shading you want. Placing your work on an angled surface will help you judge how the shading is developing. If you hold your airbrush at an angle nearly horizontal to the work and if the paper or board you are using is rough and is lying flat, the grain of the surface will produce negative shadows. By consciously exploiting this phenomenon, you can produce exciting directions and structures in your work.

Blurred Edges   If you want to produce imprecise borders of color, use a nonadhesive template (of acetate, board, or other material) and raise it up off the work with strips of masking tape or cardboard. You can control how far under the edge of the template the sprayed paint will reach by using strips of various thicknesses. If you spray between parallel rulers built up off the work, for instance, you will get blurred lines.

Balls, Circles, Ellipses, Ellipsoids   It is easy to use plexiglass templates to spray balls, circles, ellipses, and ellipsoids. Put tape over the other openings in the template and build up the under side with 1 or 2 layers of masking tape to prevent the paint from being drawn under the template by capillary action. Spray very briefly, holding the airbrush as close to vertical as possible. Let this application dry; then repeat until you have the desired coverage.

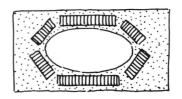

For larger circles, use a cutting inset in your compass (or a cutting compass) to cut a template out of adhesive acetate. Use a centering tack to do this. To produce shading on a ball, spray the paint with a circular motion.

Washing and Cleaning the Airbrush

As soon as you have finished spraying, spray clear water through your airbrush. If you are using oil paint or a lacquer paint that is not water soluble, use the appropriate solvent instead of water. The latter is a troublesome business, since you need a well-ventilated room. The vapors of the solvent are not too healthful. If you don't spray lacquer paint too extensively or too often, it pays to buy spray cans to escape the cleaning process. The cleaning process for the airbrush is even more effective if you cover the air jet with your finger so it sprays backwards, as it were, into the brush.

Do not take the airbrush apart to clean it unless such a total and thorough cleaning is absolutely necessary.

Stippling

Centuries ago the Japanese developed the stippling technique for transferring patterns through thin paper templates on to cloth or paper, and before silk screening became such a popular technique in the West, lettering in store windows was often produced by stippling oil paints through stencils on to the insides of the windows.

The stippling process (acrylic paint on board):

1. Cover the pencil drawing with transparent adhesive acetate; cut through all the contour lines; lift out the skin areas.
2. Stipple in the skin areas.

3. Cut and lift out the hair and dress areas; cover the skin; stipple in the hair in ocher, the dress in dark brown. The shading on the hair is done later by stippling dark brown over the ocher.

4. Cut and lift out the shape of the scarf and cover all other areas. Stipple with red. The shading of this color is done later with brown.

5. Lift off all the templates. Add detail shading with colored pencil.

155

The Paints

For stippling, the paints usually chosen are ones that are waterproof after drying: casein, resin-base paint, acrylics, and oils. Tempera, gouache, and thickly mixed watercolors and opaque watercolors can, of course, be stippled, too; but you should keep in mind that these colors are not waterproof after drying and can be either dissolved or lifted right off the page if you stipple over them. If you do use them, it is a good idea to apply a *waterproof* lacquer after each application of paint has dried. This way you can achieve a flawless final product.

Surfaces

The best material for stippling is illustration board (hot or cold press). This type of board will not warp when paint is applied to it, and because its surface is very rugged, templates can be cut out directly on it. Masonite and plywood can also be used; however, cheap papers and boards should *never* be used because masking film and Scotch tape will tear the surface and damage your painting. Make a test with tape on your board before you start.

If you want to stipple an area enclosed within lines, cover the perimeter with as wide a strip of Scotch tape as you need to prevent stippling on to a neighboring area.

The Stippling Brush

The best size stippling brush is a No. 8. Its ferrule diameter is about 2″ (5 cm), and if you always wash this brush out carefully—and do not paint stucco walls with

156

it—it will last for decades. I do not think it worthwhile to buy stippling brushes in smaller sizes because the No. 8 can be used both for large areas and for fine detail. Since most art supply stores do not have these brushes in stock, you should sketch the form of the brush for the salesperson when you order one to make sure you get what you want. You should make a point of doing this because there is another kind of long-handled stippling brush available. These brushes are graduated according to a different system. The largest one available measures only about 1″ (25 mm) in diameter, and I do not consider them as practical as those discussed in the chapter on materials.

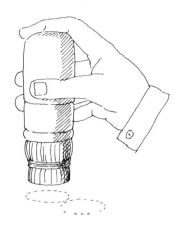

Stippling a Monotone Background

Put a rubber band around the bristles to prevent excess amounts of paint from getting into the core of the brush. The bristles will now form a compact surface ideal for stippling. Use *unthinned* paint just as it comes from the tube or jar. Paper palettes, plate glass, or porcelain plates make good surfaces for preparing the paint. Stir and work the thick paint well and remove any hard crumbs of pigment. Dip the brush lightly into the color and dab off any excess on the edge of your palette so that the paint does not drip from the brush.

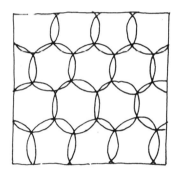

Now dab the brush on to the surface, forming one circle after another, until the whole area is covered. Try to distribute the paint so that it has a velvety appearance and no uneven mounds of color stick up in it. Continue to stipple until the brush will not give up any more paint. You can judge your results best by looking at the paint from an angle. The surface should not show any shiny (that is, damp) areas.

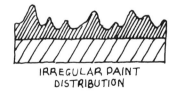

IRREGULAR PAINT
DISTRIBUTION

Do not be dismayed if the first layer does not fully cover your paper. Repeat the stippling procedure only

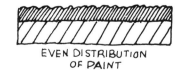

EVEN DISTRIBUTION
OF PAINT

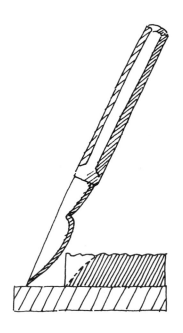

when the first application is *dry.* With the second application, stipple systematically over the entire area. If you are using casein, it may take 4 or 5 applications to get complete coverage. But the trouble you take will be well invested, for no other method apart from spraying will yield a better, more uniform underpainting than stippling.

If crumbs of paint begin to show up, the paint in the brush is too dry. Wash the brush out with soap and water, and dry it carefully with an old hand towel. Drying is important because any water left in the brush will thin the paint and cause it to run under the edges of the template. Crumbs of pigment or brush hairs that are left on the paper can be removed with a retouching knife after the work is dry. You should also round off the ridge that the relatively thick layer of paint forms on the outer perimeter of your work. Scrape it away *very carefully* with a retouching knife. This ridge can be a hindrance if you have to do additional work with a brush, colored pencil, or pen.

Other Stippling Techniques

Graphite paper 8.0
Chalk paper 8.1
Frisket 5.5
Swivel knife 6.9

Use adhesive templates to create different kinds of forms by means of shading or texturing (review the section on templates discussed under spraying at the beginning of this chapter). Stipple in the underpainting over the entire area of the work. Now add the next largest areas. To do this either you can use *pre-cut* templates with register marks, or using graphite or chalk paper, you can transfer these areas by tracing directly on to the underpainting. Now put a large piece of adhesive masking film over the areas to be stippled in, cut the marked areas out, lift them out of the film, and press the edges of the template down firmly. This cutting directly on the board should be done with a light touch so you do not cut

Comps for above stamp were stippled and executed 6 times larger than the stamp would be. Many templates for the smaller feathers were cut out of heavy tracing paper and held in place by hand during stippling. Other details were painted in by fine brushes. Completed comps for postage stamps on following page.

into the board below. Now put the increasingly smaller fields of color over the already existing fields, just as you would with opaque paints.

Fields of color can, of course, be stippled in *along-side* each other. Areas left uncovered when 2 different colors do not meet exactly should be filled in *immediately* with the color last applied. To do this, take a fine brush and thin a little of the color with water. This is essential with mixed colors, because, since impasto paints dry quickly on the palette, it would be difficult to reproduce an existing color tone with any precision. Indeed, it is a good idea to save all leftover mixed colors by wrapping them, unthinned and before they dry, in foil. They may come in handy later if you have to make any corrections in your work. (This is not necessary with unmixed colors, of course, because they can be taken from their original source at any time.)

Stippling is suitable only for painting in large areas. Lines and fine details have to be added later with pen and ink, ruling pen, or with a brush. Small fields, too, should be shaded in with a brush or colored pencil (see section later on mixed techniques).

If you want to shade an area, stipple a darker color using the same template. Start at the edge of the template and lessen the pressure on the brush as you work from the edges of the template in toward the middle. Here you can hold the brush at a slight angle so that you use only part of the brush's surface. You can use a fresh brush to do this, or you can simply dip the brush you have been using in the darker paint. By dabbing your brush into both colors on the palette, you can mix them before applying them as shading. You can produce very striking textures by applying the paint so that it does not completely cover.

Instead of buying an expensive stippling brush, you can use pieces of foam rubber of different textures and softness. They are easier to wash and dry than a brush, or just throw them away, since they aren't expensive.

Schematic representation of steel making, for an animated film by Don Stevenson (S). Stippled casein on hot-press illustration board.

Layout and Mixed Techniques

Layout

Layout is a term used in advertising. It means the sketch that shows with considerable precision what the finished work will look like. An ad or poster layout, for example, consists of sketches, usually in color, that simulate photographs or finished color drawings. The text that will be used is simulated by dummy text. Dummy text is any text chosen at random that is set up in the selected type style and size with the same spacing and overall area that the actual text in the finished work will have.

This chapter will describe how you proceed from a thumbnail sketch (your very first rough sketch) of a layout to your final artwork.

The Thumbnail Sketch

The thumbnail sketch is the simplest and cheapest sketching method. As its name suggests, the sketch can be the size of your thumbnail; it is normally not much larger than a matchbox. Working on such a small scale has the psychological value of helping you overcome the *horror vacui*, the fear we all often feel when confronted with a large, empty sheet of white paper: what to draw first, where to start—upper left-hand corner, in the middle....

The minuteness of the sketch encourages rapid composition. You can take in the whole picture and judge it in one glance. Mistakes can be quickly removed with the stroke of an eraser—whether you have a figure standing in the wrong place or one that is too large or too small, whether this proportion or that perspective is inappropriate.

The first things established in a thumbnail sketch are

Thumbnail sketch for a Leporello picture book that can be folded out to a length of 8' (240 cm). Pencil on paper, original size.

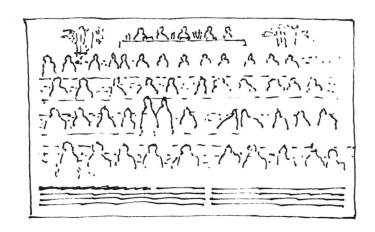

Three thumbnail sketches by Michael Preiswerk for 2-page ads in *Life* magazine size. The lines indicate where the text will go. Pen-and-ink on paper.

The finished artwork for the sketch on the top of page 164 (detail on a scale of 1:1), technical pen on paper. ▷

Liebe Freunde von Concordia Sprecher:

Seit nunmehr drei Jahren laden wir Euch auf diese persönliche Art zu uns nach Hannover ein. Und wir versuchen dort stets, Euch auch als Freunde zu empfangen. [Ihr fühlt das spätestens dann, wenn Ihr Euch in unserem Ausstellungsrahmen wohlfühlt.

Mit anderen Worten: Wir sehen in Euch - unseren Geschäftspartnern - immer zuerst >den Menschen und erst dann den Kunden<.

Das schrieben wir in der Messeeinladung vor zwei Jahren. Und das meinten wir, als wir die schöne Idee mit dem neuen Ausstellungsrahmen in die Tat umsetzten. Euch also neben unserem Produktprogramm auch so manche Entspannung präsentierten.

Nun - offensichtlich lagen wir mit dieser Idee gar nicht einmal so falsch. Denn Ihr habt Euch bei uns in Hannover doch immer sehr wohlgefühlt.

Aus diesem Grund, liebe Freunde, haben wir unseren Ausstellungsrahmen gegenüber dem letzten Jahr kaum verändert. Und darum halten wir für Euch wiederum ein kleines Angebot schöner, unterhaltsamer Dinge bereit.

Wir verweisen Euch aber auch auf eine Reihe interessanter Neuentwicklungen und Verbesserungen in unserem Produktprogramm. Wie zum Beispiel blechgeschützte Mittelspannungsanlagen, Lasttrenner-Bausteine, Niederspannungsverteilung, Betonstationen, Ableiter und einiges mehr.

Dies beweist Euch hoffentlich, daß wir von Concordia Sprecher und Sprecher+Schuh noch immer in erster Linie erfahrene Hoch-, Mittel- und Niederspannungstechniker sind. Und nicht etwa Entspannungstechniker, die nur das Vergnügen im Sinn haben.

Obwohl sich Technik und Vergnügen natürlich nicht gegenseitig ausschließen müssen. Im Gegenteil: Technik kann

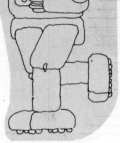

eine Menge Vergnügen betreiben. Das jedenfalls bemerken wir an uns, Technikern, wenn wir erforschen, entwickeln und zum Einsatz bringen. Und das merken wir bisweilen auch an Euch, liebe Freunde, wenn Ihr nämlich unsere Techniken erfolgreich, also zufrieden nutzt.

Wer jedoch könnte Euch diesen engen Zusammenhang zwischen Technik und Vergnügen glaubwürdiger vor Augen führen als unsere vergnügten Techniker! Lasst Euch deshalb von uns in diesem Jahr einmal auch anders überraschen. Mit einem Ding nämlich, das Euch anschaulich beweist, was in unseren Technikern steckt. Und was in unseren Schaltgeräten.

Das Ding, das Euch kennenlernen möchte, heißt Roby, beantwortet Fragen und spielt mit Euch.

166

Liebe Freunde von Concordia Sprecher.

Seit nunmehr drei Jahren laden wir Euch auf diese persönliche Art zu uns nach Hannover ein. Und wir versuchen dort stets, Euch auch als Freunde zu empfangen. (Ihr fühlt das spätestens dann, wenn Ihr Euch in unserem Ausstellungsrahmen wohlfühlt.)

Mit anderen Worten: Wir sehen in Euch - unseren Geschäftspartnern - immer zuerst »den Menschen und erst dann den Kunden«.

Das schrieben wir in der Messeeinladung vor zwei Jahren. Und das meinten wir, als wir die schöne Idee mit dem neuen Ausstellungsrahmen in die Tat umsetzten. Euch also neben unserem Produktprogramm auch so manche Entspannung präsentierten.

Nun - offensichtlich lagen wir mit dieser Idee gar nicht einmal so falsch. Denn Ihr habt Euch bei uns in Hannover doch immer sehr wohlgefühlt.

Aus diesem Grund, liebe Freunde, haben wir unseren Ausstellungsrahmen gegenüber dem letzten Jahr kaum verändert. Und darum halten wir für Euch wiederum ein kleines Angebot schöner, unterhaltsamer Dinge bereit.

Wir verweisen Euch aber auch auf eine Reihe interessanter Neuentwicklungen und Verbesserungen in unserem Produktprogramm. Wie zum Beispiel blechgeschottete Mittelspannungsanlagen, Lasttrenner-Bausteine, Niederspannungsverteilung, Betonstationen, Ableiter und einiges mehr.

Dies beweist Euch hoffentlich, daß wir von Concordia Sprecher und Sprecher + Schuh noch immer in erster Linie erfahrene Hoch-, Mittel- und Niederspannungstechniker sind. Und nicht etwa Entspannungstechniker, die nur das Vergnügen im Sinn haben.

Obwohl sich Technik und Vergnügen natürlich nicht gegenseitig ausschließen müssen. Im Gegenteil: Technik kann eine Menge Vergnügen bereiten. Das jedenfalls merken wir an uns, wenn wir Techniken erforschen, entwickeln und zum Einsatz bringen. Und das merken wir bisweilen auch an Euch, liebe Freunde, wenn Ihr nämlich unsere Techniken erfolgreich, also zufrieden nutzt.

Wer jedoch könnte Euch diesen engen Zusammenhang zwischen Technik und Vergnügen glaubwürdiger vor Augen führen als unsere vergnügten Techniker! Laßt Euch deshalb von uns in diesem Jahr einmal auch anders überraschen. Mit einem Ding nämlich, das Euch anschaulich beweist, was in unseren Technikern steckt. Und was in unseren Schaltgeräten.

Das Ding, das Euch kennenlernen möchte, heißt Roby, beantwortet Fragen und spielt mit Euch.

Sketch of an invitation to a fair by Tonci T. Pelikan. The artist took the trouble to write out the entire text just as it would later appear in print. This has the advantage that the client sees almost exactly what he will get later in print. Also, the printer will have something concrete to go by. It is quite astonishing how the finished work visually reflects the sketch right down to how the printed lines fall.

167

the dimensions within which everything will be contained. So that you will not have any surprises in the later layout stage, *always* block in your sketch in the same proportions that the finished work will have. One-sixteenth of an inch (a few millimeters) can amount to large discrepancies later on. The necessary calculations can be done by means of a simple equation:

$$\frac{\text{Width of sketch format}}{\text{Height of sketch format}} = \frac{\text{Width of finished format}}{\text{Height of finished format}}$$

This means, in practice, that once the width of the sketch has been determined, then:

$$\text{Height of the sketch} = \frac{\text{Width of sketch} \times \text{height of finished format}}{\text{Width of finished format}}$$

Calculations of this kind, which also have to be done in figuring the size of photographs, can be done with a slide rule, a proportion disk, or a pocket calculator.

Proportion disk 6.20

Use a pencil for sketching. You can leave details out, and your composition can be erased or drawn over until you are satisfied. You can also lay tracing or layout paper over your sketch and add corrections on it.

Tracing paper 3.2
Layout and visualizing paper 3.1

A thumbnail sketch provides you with a base from which you can proceed further on a given project, but it can also serve as an instruction, an explanation, or a suggestion for someone else. In short, it represents a rapidly executed means of communication that gives form to your ideas for concept, composition, proportion, perspective, and so forth.

Enlarging a Drawing

To get a preliminary layout that is proportional to your thumbnail sketch, you will have to enlarge the sketch.

Grid

With a hard pencil, draw a grid over your sketch. For small sketches, intervals can be about 1/16 to 1/8 inch.

Make sure the paper you will use for your preliminary layout has as many squares as the sketch and mark the lines with the same numbers and letters. Because of how it will be used later, this preliminary layout should be done on tracing paper. Transfer the points where the lines on the thumbnail sketch cross the grid lines on to the grid of the preliminary sketch. When you have entered these points, connect them with lines, and you have a larger sketch.

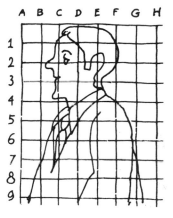

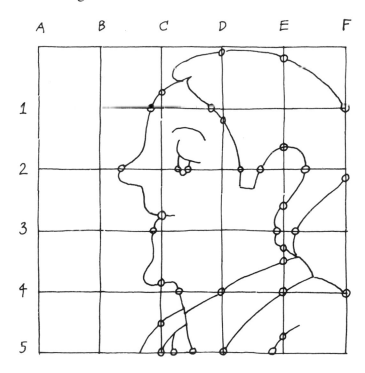

169

Photographic Enlargement

Using a fine-pointed technical pen draw your sketch on to shiny or matte acetate, lay this acetate drawing on the platform of an enlarger, and project the sketch in the size you want. If the sketch is large, you may have to copy it in 2 or more sections.

Kodak makes 35 mm slides with empty matte acetate in them. They are sold as "write-on" slides in photography shops. You can put your sketches on these slides, and then enlarge them with a slide projector. (You can make similar slides yourself by putting matte or frosted acetate in plastic slide frames.)

Story board for a TV spot by Joy Shneider (S). These sketches in felt-tipped marker are executed in shading-stroke style, some of them on the basis of photographs. The drawings convey a very exact sense of what the finished film will look like.

Opaque Projectors

Opaque projector 6.23

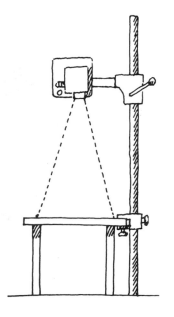

If you have to do a lot of drawing from originals, it will pay you to buy an opaque projector. Since the area in the machine for holding the original is not too large—8½"—you will have to project larger jobs in sections. Ordinarily, the device is mounted on a metal rod so it projects vertically on to a table. Most enlarging work you will do falls within the scale possible by this method, since you can make linear enlargements to 20 times the size of the original. In other words, if you have an original that is 6" (15 cm) high, the maximum enlargement will measure about 10' (3 m). For enlargements of this size, you take the machine off its metal mounting rod and make a horizontal projection on to a wall.

With these enlarging or reducing procedures, you can draw the projection directly on to your working material—paper, board, canvas—or you can make an intermediate stage on tracing paper, which can later be corrected and then transferred on to your working material. If you make the enlargement in pencil, everything can be corrected or, if you like, completely changed. Once this intermediate drawing satisfies you, you can make your final drawing right away with pen and ink or with a technical pen.

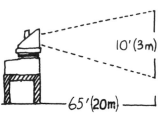

Lucy (Lucigraph)

Lucy 6.24

Another device that can be used for enlargements or reductions is what is known in advertising slang as the Lucy. With this device whose full name is Lucigraph, you place whatever it is you want to draw on a lower shelf, and the machine projects it on to a glass plate on top of the machine. The great advantage of the Lucy is that it will take opaque artwork (photos or drawings), transparencies (slides or a section of film), and even 3-dimensional objects.

Mobile Layout

Mobile layout is a method that helps you solve complex problems in a simple way. Everyone knows from his or her own experience how difficult it is to work out a large or complicated composition in drawing form. The first problem you face is where to begin: Which object will you draw first and to what size? So you wind up erasing sketches, making new ones, and erasing again.

When you find yourself in such a case, the first thing you should do is make a thumbnail sketch. Now, on paper, enlarge the figures, groups of figures, or objects to something like the size you want them to be in the finished work; trace the contours and inner details with a technical pen or a pencil, and then cut along the contours. You now have loose, mobile parts that you can move about in developing your composition.

Technical pen 1.10

Lay out the dimensions of your finished work on a large enough piece of paper and sketch in possible perspectives. Now you can move your mobile compositional elements around until they seem to be in the proper positions and perspectives. Tack them in place with a little Scotch tape or rubber cement, but do it lightly enough so they can be removed easily. If one element seems too large or too small, lay a piece of tracing paper over it, and sketch it again the size you want. Transfer this sketch to paper, cut it out, and put it in place. You can produce interim enlargements by the grid method or an enlarger, an opaque projector, a Lucy, a photostat machine (see the section on photostat process), or a zoom copier, where copies are cheaper than stats. If you are satisfied with your composition, make a fresh copy of it. However, what you have may look rather chaotic because of all the elements glued over and under each other. Add any further corrections you want, and make another fresh copy.

Rubber cement 7.1

Tracing paper 3.2

Opaque projector 6.23
Lucy 6.24
Copyproof 8.3

Copy paper 8.2

You can repeat this procedure indefinitely until you are completely satisfied with your results. Despite the additional work involved, I prefer to make still another tracing paper copy from the last copy. This last copy can consist of many mounted sketches, some enlarged (which have thicker or heavier lines), so to avoid this confusion of lines, I do the tracing paper drawing to have all lines the same strength. Then I use this copy to transfer my tracing on to my working material. In this way, I have tighter control over this final transfer.

A difference between drawing and final artwork worth noting is this: Because of the grays the lines of the

drawing produce (all the contours, the shading, the internal details, and the varying intensities of the shading strokes) all the elements in the drawing will *appear* 10 to 20% larger than they will in a finished painting. Areas between individual figures that were not particularly noticeable in the black and white drawing look like huge holes in the background of the painting. Anticipate this phenomenon either by bringing your figures closer together or by making them 10% larger on your transfer tracing sheet.

First sketch for a double-page illustration for a picture book (scale 1:1). The entire book was sketched out in this manner and then presented to the publisher. The sketches served as the basis for discussion and for the work in progress. Technical pen on glossy printing paper.

Examples of mobile elements made in different sizes from the figures in the first sketch. These elements facilitate composition.

178

Move the individual figures and groups of figures around on the background drawing (a perspective or whatever) until the composition seems balanced and correct, then stick them to the background with little strips of Scotch tape or lightly with rubber cement so that they can be easily removed if you want to make further changes. You can then make a copy from this glued-up layout. The copy is used in turn for tracing onto the working material, in this case, canvas.

179

Detail from the mobile layout and the same detail as later executed in acrylics on canvas.

Quick Perspectives

An American friend, Ed Lawing, showed us during a guest professorship the following procedure for producing a perspective drawing quickly.

Draw a horizontal line. Let's call its left end your left vanishing point (VPL), its right end, your right vanishing point (VPR). This line serves as your horizon and corresponds with the eye level of the viewer. Divide it in the middle, and label this point measuring point right (MR). Now divide the left-hand part of the line VPL-MR in half, and label this midpoint OL (object line). Finally, divide the line VPL-OL in half and label this point ML (measuring point left).

Now, from point OL, draw in the vertical axis of the drawing. This is also called the object line, and the forward edge of the object to be drawn (that is, the edge closest to the viewer) should always lie along this line. The object line then needs a scale, determined by the size of the drawing you want to make. In our example, one unit in the drawing represents 4″ (10 cm).

If the object is above eye level (or the horizon), we call that a worm's-eye view; if it is below eye level, we call that a bird's-eye view. If the top side of the object lies *above* the horizon and the bottom side under or on the horizon, we call that the frontal view or normal perspective.

Because, in our example, we want to draw a rectangular object that is 18″ (45 cm) wide, 56″ (140 cm) long, and 40″ (100 cm) high and that is standing on the ground 64″ (160 cm) below our eye level (that is, is seen from a bird's-eye view), we have to extend our object line downward from point OL.

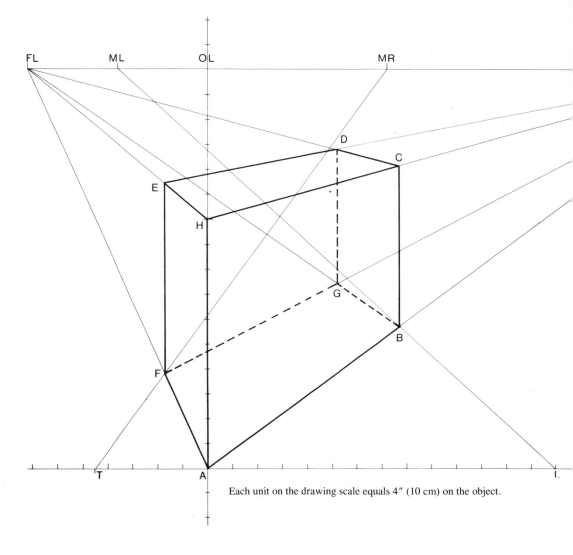

Each unit on the drawing scale equals 4″ (10 cm) on the object.

Bird's-eye view

1. Mark off 5′ (160 cm) on the vertical object line from point OL. Label this point A. From A, measure 3′ (100 cm). This gives you point H.
2. Draw the horizontal scale line through point A. Measure off 18″ (45 cm) to the left (T) and 4¹/₂′ (140 cm) to the right (L). Now join T with MR and L with ML.
3. Join the points A and H with both VPL and VPR.
4. From the junction F of the lines A - VPL and T - MR, draw a vertical line up to meet H - VPL at E. E - F is the left, rear, vertical edge of the object.
5. From the junction B of the lines L - ML and A - VPR draw a vertical line up to meet the line H - VPR at C. B - C is the right, front, vertical edge of the object.

182

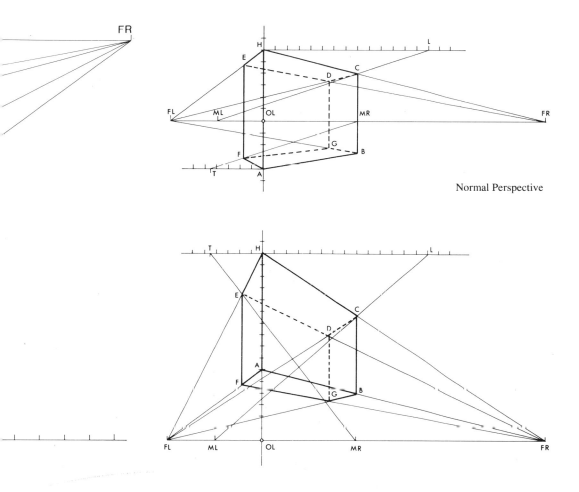

Normal Perspective

Worm's-eye view

6. Now join E with VPR and C with VPL. These lines will join at D. D-E-H-C is the upper surface of the object.

7. Join F with VPR and B with VPL. These lines cross at point G. If you join G with D, the object is now complete.

If the object is viewed from below (worm's-eye view), measure up from point OL. In normal perspective, measure off both up and down from point OL or, if the object rests on the horizon, then only upward.

183

The Pantone Matching System

The Pantone Matching System (PMS) consists of a number of products in various media with corresponding color shades. This system was developed to facilitate the graphic artist's design work and to coordinate specifications for printing.

For example, for a given colored paper, there will be a felt-tipped marker, a cover overlay, or the inks for the Letrachrome Direct Imaging or Dry Transfer processes in exactly the same color. The numbers that identify a given color in the Pantone system, of course, apply only for the Pantone system. The advantage of this system is that a certain color, whether it is produced in a felt-tipped marker, in colored paper, in a color overlay, or (in an executed design) in the Letrachrome inks, can be reproduced *exactly* by the printer when given the color number.

This correspondence in color can be guaranteed for fields of color, shading, or shading applied with screens only if there is a printer's ink that corresponds precisely with the color used in the artist's design. If, for example, a design has 6 colors, which is conceivable, for instance, in a package design, then the printer will have to have the numbers for these same 6 colors. Otherwise, the printer will work with the usual 4-color process, in which all colors are produced by overprinting the 4 basic colors (yellow, magenta, cyan, and black). The advantage of the systematized colors is that you always get the same color in the final print that you specified in your layout. This avoids disappointment later when the printed result does not reflect the artwork.

If, of course, you mix your colors, blending—let us say—colors of felt-tipped markers in shadings, then the printer will have to use the normal 4-color process to duplicate these mixes, and exact correspondence between the printed product and your artwork cannot be guaranteed. However, apart from this one exception, the Pantone Matching System has the great advantage that you can produce identical colors in the most varied of media; and this eases your design work considerably.

The Pantone Matching System includes the following media:

155 shades of broad nib felt-tipped markers and 69 fine line markers

250 color overlays: 217 full colors, 58 screen shades

603 colored papers

135 coated papers with an adhesive back

488 ink shades of the Letrachrome Direct Imaging and the Letrachrome Dry Transfer

497 printing-ink shades, based on eight basic colors

Comp for a book jacket. Watercolors and pen and ink on tinted paper. The watercolors were applied over the sepia drawing. If you use waterproof ink, the lines of the drawing will not dissolve when you apply the watercolors. To make the contrast between the drawing and the watercolors less sharp, the artist used a brown ink.

Comp for a book jacket, by Michael Keller. Pencil, watercolors, and colored pencil on watercolor paper. Watercolors were applied to the pencil drawing, then the shading was added with colored pencil.

Some Mixed Techniques

We ordinarily speak of *mixed media* if 2 or more techniques are combined in a single work. For example, you can do your underpainting in tempera and paint over that with oils. However, included in that category should be different techniques of application for the same medium, for example, spraying the ground with casein or acrylics and then adding the detailed work in these same paints with a fine brush. A dozen varied techniques are described here.

Detail from the Leporello picture book (pages 100-10). The line drawing was printed in brown ink onto watercolor paper and then colored with watercolor and shaded with color pencils.

Page from a reader.

The drawing was done in black ink. It was then printed onto the watercolor board in blue printer's ink, which does not appear in the 4-color reproduction. A wash in liquid watercolor was then applied over the print, and the watercolor was reproduced. After this, the drawing was stripped in as line art into the screened black film in the 4-color process. The result is solid, unscreened lines that stand out sharply on the color. Ordinarily, the lines of the watercolor drawing would have been screened, too, and hence have lost their sharpness.

Film poster by Jörg Huber. Mixed technique on illustration board, 22″ × 31″ (55.5 × 78.5 cm). Gouache was applied over casein-base priming (a casein emulsion with pigmentation, made by the artist). Between the primer and the gouache, there are various layers of casein and watercolor washes applied with an airbrush.

Pencil Drawing and Watercolors   Unlike pen and ink, a pencil drawing creates a soft contrast to the watercolors. It can be done with thin, pale lines or thick, heavy ones. But, depending on the type of watercolors you use, a pencil drawing cannot always be erased after you have applied your watercolors. Try a sample first to be sure.

Pencils 1.0, 1.1, 1.2
Watercolors 2.6, 2.19

Pen-and-ink Drawing and Watercolors   It is best to use waterproof ink because otherwise the wet watercolor brush can dissolve the lines and that will darken your colors. The contrast between the drawing and the watercolors can be softened by using a colored ink, such as sepia.

Drawing inks 1.8, 1.9, 2.23

Watercolors 2.6, 2.19

Fields of Colored Ink Combined with Watercolors   You can use waterproof colored inks to paint areas of color that will then be painted over with watercolors. Then inks will not be affected by the water, and if you wash the watercolors to make them paler, the ink will retain its original intensity of color.

Colored inks 2.23
Watercolors 2.6, 2.19

Fields of Watercolor as Underpainting for Colored Pencil Drawing   Watercolors applied in fields of color make a good base for working in flat areas of colored pencil. See, too, the earlier section on colored pencils.

Watercolors Shaded with Colored Pencil   Watercolored surfaces can be quickly shaded or blended with colored pencils. Colored pencils can also be used for contour lines and interior details.

Watercolors over Pen-and-ink Drawing, Shaded with Colored Pencils   This is a combination of 2 techniques described above.

Painted, Stippled, or Sprayed Casein Fields Combined with Watercolors   Once the waterproof casein is dry, you can add watercolors over it: lines with a pen, large areas with a brush, as well as shadings with an airbrush.

Casein 2.11
Watercolors 2.6, 2.19

Bird painting by Karin Weber(S).

The body was stippled in with casein; the details, like the feathers, were added with a very fine brush. The artist began with the dark areas and finished with the light ones.

Painted, Stippled, or Sprayed Casein Fields Shaded with Colored Pencils Shading and details in colored pencil can be added more easily to a stippled or sprayed area than they can to a painted one.

Colored pencils, leads 2.0, 2.1

Mixed techniques by Elke Baier (S). Acrylic paint and colored pencil on cold-press illustration board. The fields of color are stippled in with acrylic and the darker nuances shaded in with colored pencils. The highlights were added with either white or light-colored pencils.

Painted, Stippled, or Sprayed Casein Fields Painted over with Opaque Paints, Gouache, or Tempera These paints can be applied in transparent or opaque density over the waterproof casein.

Opaque watercolors 2.8
Gouache 2.7
Tempera 2.9

Stippled or Sprayed Casein Fields Shaded or Detailed with a Fine Brush You can add color fields, shading, and dots with a fine brush. See, too, the earlier section on opaque paints.

Acrylic Paints: Shading and Details Added as in the Last 4 Techniques Described Above Here, acrylic paints are used instead of casein.

Acrylic Modeling Paste Combined with Thinned Acrylic Paint Modeling Paste applied as is or mixed with sand and applied with a spatula can be painted over with very diluted acrylics. The paint penetrates the surface only lightly, and you can go over the same area many times until you can achieve the tone you want.

Painting on Acetate

Most animations for film and television are drawn or painted on acetate. Since 1 second in an animated film may need as many as 24 individual pictures, the sequences of movements require a transparent working material because every change is based on the previous picture. Because backgrounds rarely change in animated films, they can be built up with watercolors, tempera, casein, or acrylics on paper or board. However, all the movable parts, such as people, animals, cars, and even, on occasion, entire foregrounds, are drawn and painted on acetate. The process of painting on acetate is essentially like reverse glass painting (*hinterglasmalerei*), that is, working in reverse from foreground to

Scene from the animated film *The Wonderlamp* by Don Stevenson (submitted as an exam project). The hall was carefully painted in watercolors. The figures were drawn on animation film acetate, then painted in on the reverse side with acetate paint. To create the impression of greater depth, the artist laid a light gray acetate between the figures and the background. Acetates of different colors can be used in this way to create various atmospheres.

194

background, and it differs only in the material used. Even in the very elaborate Walt Disney animations, which have unusually detailed and plastic backgrounds, the movable parts, that is, the figures, are *never* shaded but only drawn in contour. Then the areas within the lines are filled in with color. Since shadows follow the form of the body, they consist of constantly changing shadings. This would make shading in animated films a demanding, time-consuming, and therefore hugely expensive proposition, so normally it is not used.

Putting figures and foreground objects on acetate for film or television work has a further advantage: the background can be pulled out from under the figures, thus making changes quick and easy.

The Procedure

Acetate 5.0

Wash the acetate with dishwashing detergent to remove all oils and fingerprints; only an acetate that is free of oils will take paints uniformly. This is why you should also lay a sheet of paper between your hand (in a white, lint free cotton glove) and the acetate when you are painting. Lay the acetate on your preliminary drawing Technical pen 1.10 and trace the drawing using a technical pen with a stroke width between .35 and .7 mm, or sizes 000 to 2. Once the lines are dry, turn the acetate over and put your paints on the *back*.

The following paints can be used:

Tempera 2.9
Gouache 2.7   1. Tempera or gouache
Casein 2.11   2. Casein
Acrylic paint 2.13   3. Acrylics
Photo Ace 2.22   4. Opaque paints with Flex-Opaque (Dr. Martin's) added.

Flex-Opaque makes paints adhere to acetate and other glossy surfaces.

196

Because tempera and gouache are very sensitive, and opaque paints with the additive complicated to use, I prefer casein and acrylics for acetate work. The quality of color they produce is intense and uniform. In commercial animation studios in the United States, however, gouache is preferred, usually premixed in quantity to their standard specifications.

If using casein, the paint should not be mixed too thin, for the first application should cover. However, some colors require several applications. The paint layer should not be ridged or have brushstrokes in it, because the ridge lifts the acetate cell slightly off the background and causes the hairline shadow edges in camera.

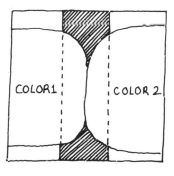

The lines made with the technical pen have the same function as the lead framing in a stained glass window—providing borders for color. Apply your paint up to the middle of a line; then bring the second color from the other side of the line up to the first color. The heavier the lines, the easier job of painting. Because acetate tends to bend up off the table and so make painting it difficult, press it down with a pencil or something else held in your free hand. Now and then you should lift the acetate up and look through it to see whether the colors touch the lines everywhere. You can then fill in blank spaces immediately.

Corrections in either casein or acrylics can be made only by scraping the paint away with a brush handle that has been sharpened with a knife, because the paints cannot be dissolved with water once they have dried. Be very careful when scraping because the acetate scratches easily. If large corrections have to be made, it is better to redo the whole procedure.

Cutting and Pasting

Cutting Paper and Boards

Silhouette scissors 6.11

The most important thing to use for cutting paper and board is sharp tools. For paper, the 2 types of scissors described in the chapter on materials are quite adequate. For fine details, use the silhouette scissors, so-called because of their use for cutting out silhouettes. For all other tasks, regular office scissors will do; I have found the large scissors often called *paper scissors* very unwieldy, impractical, and imprecise. Anything you cannot cut out with extremely precise office scissors you had best do with a knife. If you have to make a lot of right-angle cuts, you should get a solidly built paper cutter with a blade a foot long or more.

Utility knife 6.8
Cutting straight edge 1.24

To make a cutting board, you need a cardboard base, a sturdy utility knife, and a cutting ruler. The best cutting rulers are aluminum with an inlaid steel cutting edge and a rubber strip on the bottom to prevent slipping. These rulers are much preferable to all-steel ones. You can, of course, cut along the edge of any acrylic ruler, but you should not expect to be able to cut a straight line along the edge of such a ruler after it has been used for a while.

Cutting Mats

A mat is a frame for a piece of artwork that is usually made of either cardboard or paper. Using a light pencil line, draw the dimensions you want on the back of the material. This way, you will not have to to any erasing. Be sure to put a cheap piece of cardboard under your work to prevent your knife from cutting into the work table and from getting prematurely dull. Hold the ruler so that the knife side is always on the inside of the frame. Therefore if the knife should slip, it will only cut into the center part that will be taken out. In cutting thick boards, you should *never* try to press down hard. The first cut along the ruler should merely scratch the paper and make the groove for the knife to run in. Pressing lightly, cut along the ruler repeatedly until the board is cut through. Using this procedure, you will get perfectly straight lines, provided that the knife is really sharp. Once you have cut along all 4 sides, smooth the edges with a burnisher, because the cutting of thick boards produces razor-sharp edges that stand up and can easily cut you.

A mat not only covers edges that can be, for any number of reasons, messy and inexact, but it also heightens the impact of the work. In fact, the wider the mat, the quieter the surrounding area is for the eye and the better it can focus on the center, namely, the work itself. If you want to protect your work from spatterings of water, fingerprints, dust, or accidental injury, stick a sheet of acetate either on the back of the mat or directly on the work with Scotch tape.

Now stick a strip of double-sided tape or regular tape on the upper edge of the mat *from inside* so that the tape cannot be seen. This tape also makes it possible to raise the mat if you want to make any corrections later. You should not glue the mat down on all 4 sides. If you do not want the mat to be raised, 2 small pieces of double-sided tape on the bottom edge will suffice. Another method is to use masking tape all around (for protection) for presentations or to use paper tape for a permanent mount.

Your work should always have enough of a margin on it so that you can attach a mat over it. If the work is on a very thin board or paper, either fasten it on a heavy piece of board to which a mat can be fastened, or make a fold-up mat, as described above, using board as the

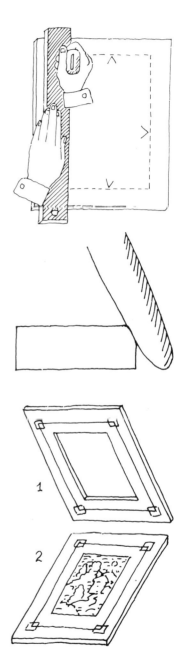

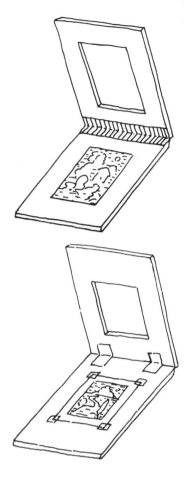

backing and adding a frame. Put your work in this mount and fasten it lightly with acid-free tape. (You should never use Scotch tape or rubber cement with originals or valuable graphics.)

Mat board will do for most purposes. However, depending on how you want to present your work and on what purpose you have in mind for it, you may want to choose heavier, more expensive boards. A good piece of work deserves a complimentary frame. It should add to the effect of the work, not detract from it.

Mounting Papers and Photographs

Mounting is what we call the process of gluing paper, photographic paper, board, or any other material you choose on a background that is itself paper, board, Masonite, plywood, or some other material. The trick is to do this without leaving any bubbles or wrinkles. Drafts on thin paper especially can be presented to advantage in this way. Mounting is therefore most often used as a means of presenting and exhibiting your work.

Mounting with Rubber Cement

Cut a 2½" x 4" (6 x 10 cm) piece of Bristol board or some other kind of board or plastic to use as a spatula. Apply a strip of rubber cement to the back of the paper to be mounted and, using the spatula, spread the first strip of cement, then a second, third, and so on, down to the bottom of the paper. The layer of cement can be very thin. The important thing is that you leave no empty places. You can check for them by looking at the paper from an angle. Now apply rubber cement to the mounting board in the same way, spreading the cement over the entire surface. Once both surfaces are dry, carefully place the upper edge of the paper on the upper edge of the board, holding the lower edge of the paper up. Now

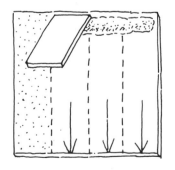

slowly lower the paper, smoothing it constantly with your free hand so that no bubbles or wrinkles can form. Finish up by laying a large sheet of scrap paper over the mounting and rubbing the entire area down firmly once more. However, do not do this final step if you are working with valuable prints, because chemical reactions among the rubber cement, the paper, and the printing ink could cause discolorations and other damage after a certain amount of time.

For quick mounting, when it is not essential that the cement cover the entire surface, the following procedure is quite adequate. Apply the cement in a zigzag pattern to the back of the paper to be mounted, place the paper where you want it, and lay a larger sheet of paper over it to protect it. Then, starting at the middle and working out toward the edges, roll it firmly with a rubber roller. This spreads the cement out in a very thin layer. Any cement that is pressed out at the edges of the mounted paper can be removed with a rubber eraser. With small items, such as lines of print, you can dispense with the roller. Just wiggle the strip of paper back and forth a bit on the mounting board to spread the cement evenly on it, position the strip where you want it, then press down on it firmly.

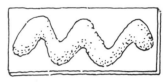

Mounting lettering and small pieces of paper is done today with rubber cement or wax. I find rubber cement the handiest because it can be applied quickly and cleanly.

Some advantages of rubber cement are:

1. The items to be cemented together remain movable longer than with cements like Duco.
2. The parts can be separated again after the cement is dry (although care is required with very thin papers). Lift a corner of the paper carefully with a retouching knife and then slowly peel the paper back.
3. Excess cement can be simply rubbed away with your finger or with a pick-up, or you can pour thinner on it and peel it off.

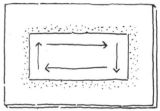

Pick-up 7.3

Poster by Seymour Chwast. A considerable portion of Chwast's recent work combines line art with tinted overlays. The drawing is done in gray lines that, in the bicycle and its rider, widen out into fields of gray or in some areas appear black because of the overlays used with them. The use of overlays (in this case, Cell-opak overlays) always guarantees uniform shades of color and makes drafting easier because inappropriate colors can simply be exchanged for others.

Collage in colored papers by Gabriele Heid (S). The different colored papers are mounted with rubber cement.

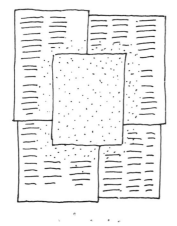

Mounting with Spray Adhesives

The sale of aerosol sprays was prohibited for a while, but now they are on the market again. They may well be forbidden again because of the harmful propellant gases used in them.

This adhesive is sprayed on only one of the surfaces to be glued together, usually on the photograph or paper to be mounted. Lay the item back side up on some newspapers and spray it. Pick the sprayed item up carefully, hold it in both hands, turn it over, and lay its upper edge on the mounting board. Now, with a single movement from top to bottom, press it on to the board. Work slowly so that you are sure to squeeze out all bubbles and wrinkles. If necessary, roll it with a rubber roller. Because this adhesive is very strong, you will be able to separate the 2 pieces only as long as the adhesive is still fresh. There is also 3m Scotch Spray Mount, which could be used when the parts need to be separated again and again. This spray is preferable in layout work because items have to be removed and positioned anew.

Excess adhesive can be removed with a few drops of cleaning or lighter fluid on a paper towel. Do not dampen the towel too much, or the solvent may creep under the cemented edge and remove the adhesive.

Mounting with Double-Coated Tapes and Other Adhesive Materials

Double-coated tape 7.7

Double-coated foil, available in roll form, is usually used for mounting photographs. The foil consists of a thin layer of adhesive on a protective paper. After you have carefully unrolled the foil (it will stick to your fingers instantly and persistently!), lay the reverse side of your photograph on the adhesive layer and cut around it. Press down again to make sure that the adhesive layer is sticking firmly and is free of bubbles. Now pull off the protective paper and, starting at one corner, lay the photo on the mounting board, finishing the mounting process as you would with rubber cement or spray adhesive.

Mounting with Dry Mount

Although dry mount can be used to cement paper and board together, it is usually used only for mounting photographs. It is available as a light, fragile, paperlike material that comes in rolls and is covered with a protective paper. Under normal conditions and temperatures, dry mount is not sticky.

Cut the dry mount somewhat larger than the photo to be mounted and place it between the photo and the mounting board. Now put a covering sheet of paper over the whole thing and run a hot flatiron over it. The heat softens the adhesive, and when the adhesive cools, it hardens and glues the 2 pieces together. If you have to do many mountings of this kind, there are presses available in which you can lay these "sandwiches" and do several at one time. To make this process easier, you can tack the dry mount to the back of the photo by touching it at 2 to 4 points with a warm electrical soldering iron. This way, the photo is prevented from sliding around on the dry mount. Each piece can then be ironed and trimmed.

Dry mount 7.8

Collages and Colored Paper

Pasting pieces of colored paper, printing, photographs, and other materials on a surface—often one over another—is a form of composition known as *collage*. There are 2 kinds of colored papers you can use. Either the entire mass of the paper is dyed, as with handmade watercolor or tone papers, so the back of the paper is the same color as the front. Or they have the color printed or applied to only one side, as in Color-Aid and Pantone papers. Both kinds can be used quickly and cleanly to produce fields of color. The color tones are always constant and can be matched at will.

Handmade watercolor paper 4.2
Colored paper 4.6
Tinted paper 4.4

205

The Procedure

Since the tone on the papers colored on only one side will often not stand up to erasing, always transfer your contour lines on to the *back* of the paper. Depending on the size of the piece you want to cut, use either silhouette or regular scissors.

Poster for an educational TV program. The individual elements in the poster are the emblems of the book covers to be used in the educational series. The emblems are made of cut-outs from colored paper mounted with rubber cement.

In this procedure, cut out the largest background area first. On the front of this piece, mark very lightly the position of the next smallest piece and cement this in place with rubber cement. Mark and glue the ever smaller pieces in this fashion, so the structure of the collage looks like an architect's relief model, one layer lying on top of another.

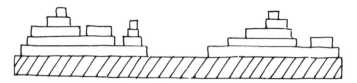

If there are small fields of background color in the finished collage, you can avoid cutting these out of every new layer you add simply by gluing small patches of the background color *on top* of the finished collage. Fields of color that border each other do not have to be cut out to fit against each other exactly. The upper layer, cut precisely to size, will cover an oversized neighboring field.

Rubber cement is the appropriate adhesive to use here for a clean, trouble-free job, unless you want a permanent piece of art. (Rubber cement damages artwork over time.) Apply it to large areas (as described above). For small pieces, apply a drop straight from the brush; then spread the cement by rubbing the piece into its place on the background. The cement should form a very *thin* layer on both surfaces and be absolutely dry when you actually press the pieces together. For this reason, you should put the paper in place and lift one side up to dry. When it is dry, press it down firmly in its final position and then lift the other side up to dry. If the cement is still *damp* when you glue your pieces together, the solvent may bleed through the paper, causing spots and changes in color.

JOINT

Using Color Overlays

Color overlays 5.1 The application of color overlays is a much favored method for coloring line drawings and other graphic representations because it is both clean and quick.

The overlays are self-adhering, transparent (so that you can see lines through them), and available in a wide range of the subtlest color tones. By applying them over each other, you can also produce new tones. That is, add diverse overlays over your base color until you achieve a harmonious combination of colors. Tones that clash can easily be pulled out. This procedure opens up tremendous creative possibilities for developing new and unusual color combinations.

The Procedure

Bristol board 3.4

Make your drawing on heavy paper or board with a technical pen, pen and ink, brush and ink or whatever. Now place the overlay sheet with its protective paper on the drawing and draw a rough outline around the figure to be colored (see drawing at right). Cut around the outline with your scissors and pull off the protective paper. Now lightly press the cut-out overlay on to the board, and using light pressure, cut along the contour lines, using an acetate cutter with a movable blade. (Use a fixed blade for straight lines.)

You will inevitably cut into the board, because even if you cut as carefully as you can, you still have to cut all the way through the overlay. For this reason, illustration board (hot press) is recommended as a background. Lift off the edge, and then lay a piece of protective paper over your work and rub the overlay down firmly.

If the work will eventually be printed by the 4-color offset process, you will encounter the following problem: The lines of the drawing will also be screened into dots and therefore lose their sharpness. If you want to avoid this, make your drawing on the board with a hard, thin, pencil, so the lines are just visible through the color overlay to allow you to cut out the contours. After you have cut out your overlays, put a piece of transparent acetate over the finished work and trace over your line drawing with a pen or technical pen so that the pencil lines and the color borders are covered. This acetate drawing will then be photographed on high-contrast film and stripped in on the black film. In this way, you get precise line definition around your fields of color when the work is printed. This is called a *perfect trap line*.

Acetate 5.0
Technical pen 1.10

Another possibility is to put your drawing on an overlay sheet over which you lay transparent acetate with register marks. On this acetate you now strip in your color overlays. When you are all done, you then put the sheet with the line drawing on top of it, for the presentation.

If you want to cut a circle out of overlay material or paper, replace the pencil insert in your compass with the knife insert and draw your circle with light pressure as often as is needed to cut through the acetate. Use a centering tack in the middle of the circle to prevent the compass from creating a large hole in the board and so making it impossible to cut an exact circle.

Cutter blade or cutter compass
1.16 or 1.17

There are 2 possible ways to apply color with color overlays:

1. The overlays can be placed next to each other, and then every field of color consists of only one layer of overlay.
2. The overlays can be placed on top of each other. Shading, color mixtures, and variations of tone are produced by several layers of the same or different colors. As with collages, remember to apply the smallest parts of the work last.

Using Screen and Pattern Overlays

Monotone black screens are used in drawings to create surfaces, depth, gradations, or accents. In newspaper advertisements, which are printed only in black and white, the gradations of the screens take over the function of color or the halftones.

These self-adhering screens are used in the same way as the color overlays just described. As you actually practice graphic techniques, you will often encounter separate screens placed alongside each other. However, more sophisticated effects can be achieved by laying screens of the same or different patterns over each other. This can produce new patterns, moirés, or plastic effects. On the following pages, you will see some patterns illustrating how different types of screens can be combined at various angles to create certain effects.

Contact Copying Machines

Contact copying machine 6.25

A contact copying machine consists of 2 parts: a contact-exposure unit and a built-in developing device. With this developing device you can develop not only contact materials but also the highly sensitive papers and films designed for reprocameras. However, these latter materials can be developed *only* in a darkroom (see The Copyproof Photostat Process, page 236). If you own a contact copying machine of this type, you can spare yourself the expense of buying a developing machine for your reprocamera (see page 237).

Copyproof materials 8.2

Copyproof materials for repro camera 8.3

With this machine you can make only one copy (contact) at a time, and the copy will be the same size as the original. The machine uses a liquid stabilizer (CP 296B),

Illustration by Frank Elter for a short story by Wolfdietrich Schnurre (S). The striking plasticity of the tank was achieved in a very simple way with the use of only 1 line screen. By slight shiftings in the angle of the base screen, the illustrator creates an effect usually achieved with a progression screen.

Creating plasticity by laying
simple line screens over each
other at slight angles.

Left-hand column: LT 211
Right-hand column: LT 77

2 layers, overlaid at slight angle

3 layers, overlaid at slight angle

4 layers, overlaid at slight angle

212

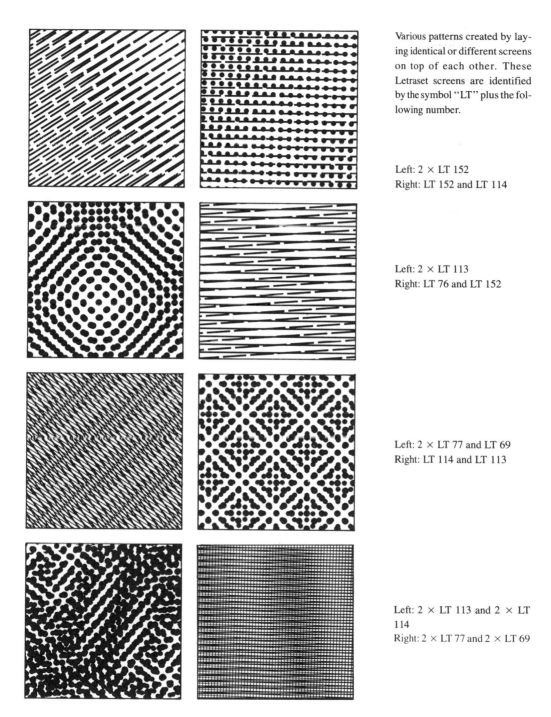

Various patterns created by laying identical or different screens on top of each other. These Letraset screens are identified by the symbol "LT" plus the following number.

Left: 2 × LT 152
Right: LT 152 and LT 114

Left: 2 × LT 113
Right: LT 76 and LT 152

Left: 2 × LT 77 and LT 69
Right: LT 114 and LT 113

Left: 2 × LT 113 and 2 × LT 114
Right: 2 × LT 77 and 2 × LT 69

213

The representation of balls with overlays of identical dot screens. The upper row shows the basic screens used; the examples below it show the same screens used in 2, 3, and 4 layers.

Left-hand column: LT 1 (10%)
Right-hand column: LT 4 (40%)

2 layers, slightly misaligned

3 layers, slightly misaligned

4 layers, slightly misaligned

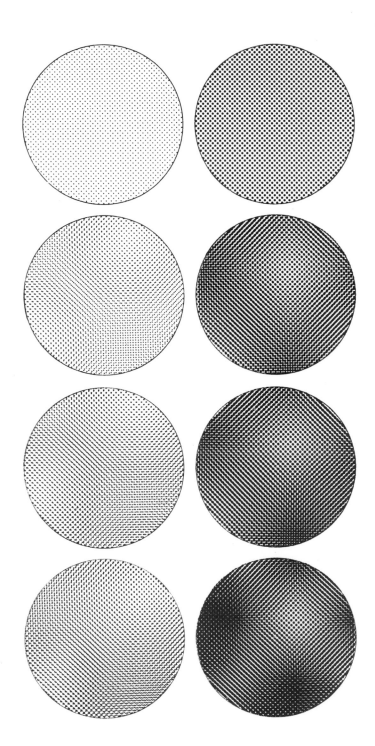

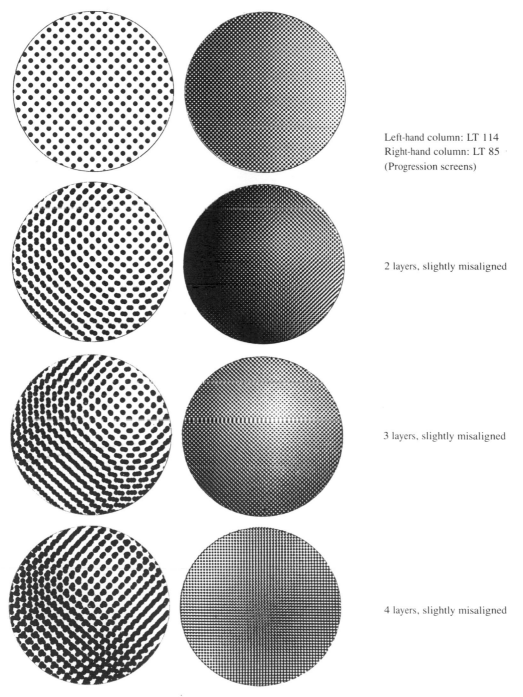

Left-hand column: LT 114
Right-hand column: LT 85
(Progression screens)

2 layers, slightly misaligned

3 layers, slightly misaligned

4 layers, slightly misaligned

215

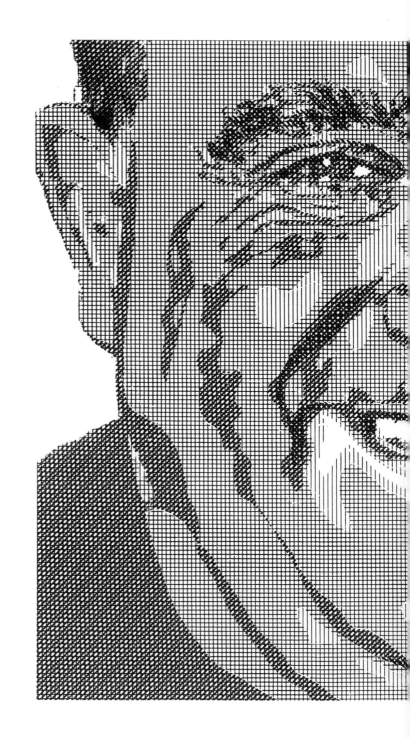

216

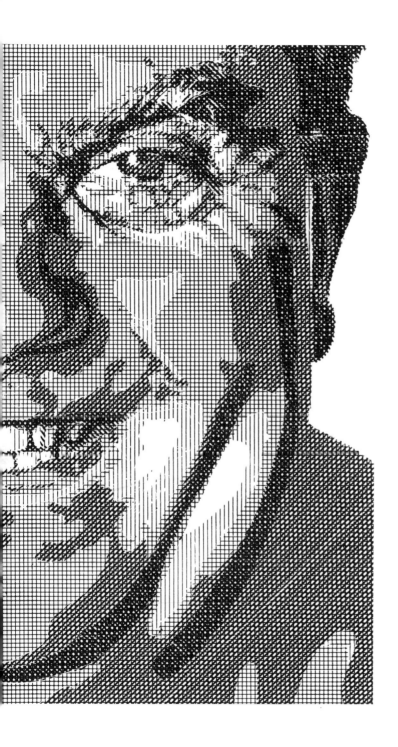

Translation of an original into crosshatching with the use of a single line screen. Term project by Karin Weber. The first layer was done with the lines of the screen placed vertically. The white areas were then cut out. The second gradation of gray was produced by laying the screen lines at a right angle to those in the first layer; the third, at a 45° angle; the last, at a 135° angle.

which is both developer and fixative at once. For each print, you need 1 sheet of negative paper (CPC) and 1 sheet of positive (CPP). When compared with a normal dry-copy machine, with which you can make as many copies as you want and copy on various kinds of paper as well as on colored papers, working this machine sounds awkward indeed. However the possibilities I describe later can otherwise be achieved only with a lot of time-consuming darkroom work, and with dry copiers of the current type they cannot be achieved at all. If you decide to buy a contact copying machine, get one with a built-in electrical vacuum pump. The negative material (CPC) is only slightly sensitive to light, and you can therefore dispense with a darkroom. You should, however, avoid strong sunlight or artificial light. The darker your workroom is, the richer in contrast your copies will be. Your negative paper should be stored away from light.

There are 2 methods you can use with a contact copying machine: photostat copying and back-light copying. Let's examine each.

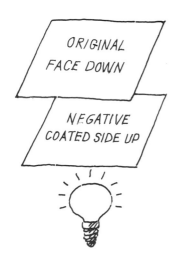

Photostat Copying
Photostat copying is used with material that is either not transparent (for example, photographs or drawings mounted on board) or that has printing or artwork on its reverse side (such as material from books or magazines). There can be practically no variation in exposure time in photostat copying. The exposure has to fall between 11 and 13 seconds (marks 11 and 13 on the timer), while in back-light copying, the exposure can be anywhere between 11 seconds and 8 or more minutes.

Back-light Copying
With back-light copying you can work with transparent and translucent materials, such as film, acetate, tracing paper, thin paper, paper-thin photographs, and so on. The exposure time can vary greatly.

One advantage of the contact copying machine is the thorough blacking-in of dots, lines, and dark fields. Anything dark turns out a deep black. Depending on exposure time, the tones in photographs become variegated fields of pure black or pure white. Thus, a pencil line will become either a black line, or it will be broken up into dots and line segments. By changing the exposure time, you can make the dark sections of an original appear thicker or thinner: *Longer* exposure makes a line thinner; *shorter* exposure makes a line thicker. There are, of course, limits that you cannot overstep in both these directions. The possibilities are rich indeed, however, and you will often achieve results you could not have predicted.

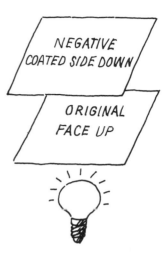

From halftone originals—photos and drawings on thin paper—you can make line conversion copies and screens at varying levels of intensity, provided, of course, that your originals are translucent enough and that the reverse sides are blank. If a photograph has indelible writing or a stamp on the back, you can try to use a solvent or scrape it off very carefully with a razor blade. However, be sure not to scrape the paper too thin, because thin spots can let too much light through and also make blemishes in your copy.

The Copying Process

Lay the original and the negative paper together on the glass plate of the contact copier. If you are photostat copying, place the sheets in the order shown in the illustration on page 218. If you are back-light copying, use the order shown above. Now close the cover of the copier and, as soon as the vacuum frame is tight, expose the material. The exposed negative and a sheet of positive paper are now shoved—the coated sides of both sheets facing each other—into their respective slots in the

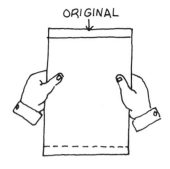

ORIGINAL

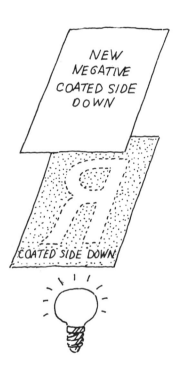

NEW
NEGATIVE
COATED SIDE
DOWN

COATED SIDE DOWN

developing section of the machine. The lower paper should be inserted with a lead of about $\frac{1}{8}''$ (2 to 3 mm). If this is done correctly, the 2 papers will come out of the machine exactly face to face. If you hold the work up to the light, you will be able to see the progressive darkening take place. When this developing process is over (after about twenty seconds), you can separate the negative and the print. Since warmth speeds up the developing process, you can pass the 2 sheets, while they are still together, slowly back and forth in front of a warm-air blower. The blower can also be used to dry off the damp print.

Copy paper yellows after a while, particularly if it is exposed to a lot of sunlight. But because these copies are usually used only as short-term working copies (for layout purposes or as preliminary stages in a drawing or printing process), their short life is of no great disadvantage. To make your positives more durable, you can fix them with Offset Fixer CR 6108.

As a rule, the used negative paper is not of any further value, and you will throw it away. However, it can be used for reversing work, as in making negative lettering. To do this, expose it with its coated side to the light (that is, just reverse the normal position). The contours will not be very sharp, but copies made this way are quite adequate for layout work.

Converting from a Halftone Print to Line Art

A line art conversion (or outline conversion) is a photographic conversion of a halftone original into so-called line art; that is, into pure black-and-white fields, lines, and dots (which are actually fields, too).

220

Back-lit copy by Michael Keller. Two identical, screen copies were laid one on top of the other and slightly off center to produce this moiré effect.

222

Manipulation of line strength by varying exposure time. The first picture on the far left is a copy of a pencil drawing back-lit for 13 seconds. With this exposure time, the lines in the original and in the copy are of the same thickness. (All the exposure data given here are taken from my copying machine, but because the effects of different exposure times vary from machine to machine, I offer the data from my machine only as a basis of comparison.) From this first copy I made a second copy, again back-lit but with a shorter exposure (10 seconds). This second copy shows markedly heavier lines. Keeping the exposure time at 10 units, I continued making new copies from the preceding ones until I reached the thickness of line I wanted (third picture). The details in the center row are from double enlargements of the pictures above them. The details in the bottom row are from quadruple enlargements. These details illustrate how shading lines blend together into areas of solid color in this process and how lines become more interesting by growing heavier.

The picture on this page is a double enlargement of Picture 3 on page 222.

Photo by Michael Keller.

Depending on the exposure time, a gray halftone field will become either black or white. In the example shown here, you can easily observe this process in the crushed car door where the strong shadows of the deformed metal visible in the second and third prints disappear completely in the prints with longer exposures. In the last print, the structure of the brick work almost completely disappears due to overexposure, but the writing on the wall, which is as dark as the tires, becomes visible here for the first time. In these line conversions grayish areas come out as more or less variegated fields of black.

224

35"

55"

1'15"

1'55"

226

2′ 35″

4′

Screen Overlaying

Screen overlay 5.2
Clear acetate 5.0

Use the back-light copying method for screen overlaying. To do this, you need a screen that is on acetate and that can be laid either *over* or *under* the original with the screen coating facing up. Ideal for this purpose are non-adhesive screens. Letraset or Mecanorama screens mounted on transparent acetate will also do very well here. The longer you expose these screens, the more the screen dots or lines will be overilluminated. The result is that they fade and even disappear completely in those

Overlaying of a pencil drawing with a mezzotint screen. The numbers give the exposure units used for back lighting each print.

10'

13'

15'

18'

23'

30'

229

Screen overlaying of a photograph, using a line screen. Silk-screen original for the Surface Transportation Division of the German Museum, Munich.

Here the entire original was broken down into lines; and the blacks, grays, and light grays of the original are reflected by heavy, thin, or broken lines. This effect can be seen clearly in the enlargement. The observer's eye fills in the missing details, such as the upper edge of the tire and the right half of the chauffeur's face.

230

areas where the original showed white or light gray. Black or dark gray areas, after long exposures, no longer appear as fields of solid color but instead show the pattern of the screen being used.

In summary, contact copying machines give you the following advantages:

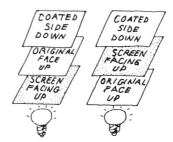

1. Uniform black coloration. Dots, lines, and fields come out deep black and show precision contours.
2. The cut edges from overlaid layers, tape, corrections made with opaque white or liquid paper, and pencil marks made with very hard, fine, or light blue pencils do not show up on the copies. This is very useful for layouts and presentations.
3. Line conversions and screen conversions can be done easily and without intermediate steps.
4. All procedures can be executed in a matter of a few minutes.

These advantages have to be considered in relation to what is required to get comparable results using darkroom techniques or other copying machines.

The illustrations on these pages were made with the Autotype Artsystem. The manufacturer has discontinued this product without explaining his reasons for taking it off the market. However, the same can be achieved with Letrachrome and Chromatec; and because the results are identical, I have retained these sample illustrations.

232

 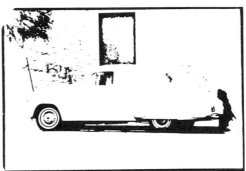

233

Other Copying Machines

The industry has developed a number of machines for office use that are considerably more expensive than the contact copying machine and that have their own particular advantages. Some of them will make copies on any kind of paper including colored papers and acetates. These copies can then be worked on with colored pencils, felt-tipped markers, and watercolors. Thus, a wide range of possibilities is opened up.

Colored pencils 2.0
Felt-tipped markers 2.5
Watercolors 2.6, 2.19
Photo Ace 2.22

Other copiers can use only a special paper, but those machines have the advantage of producing better half-tone quality. There are color-copying processes now which allow you to use almost every sort of paper, on which the copy can be made. This indeed opens wide the possibilities for creative work in many fields. Since the paper itself could be a colored one, the variations are immense. For most up-to-date information on such developments, speak with informed salespersons in copy shops.

This series of line screenings (also back-lit) shows how light areas such as the headlights are soon transformed into white. If you wanted to use the fourth version, you would have to cut the headlights out of the first or second version and mount them with rubber cement. Exposure times, from 1 to 10 minutes.

Copies laid one over another and back-lit. Here a high-contrast copy was made of a halftone original. Then 5 copies were made of the high-contrast copy. Finally, the 6 copies were placed on top of each other and back lit.

Copyproof Photostat Process and the Reprocamera

Copyproof materials 8.3

A photostat is a print, on paper or film, made with a *paper negative.* The materials—marketed by Agfa under the name Copyproof—have to be processed under a ceramic covered red bulb in a darkroom. (A good darkroom light is the Philip's Red Neon Light by Illumination Technology, Inc. This light illuminates the entire darkroom, making it much easier to work because the light spreads much farther.) The exposure is made in a stat camera, with which you can make exact enlargements and reductions. Developing and stabilizing are done simultaneously; the process is similar to that of the contact (or wet) copying machine (see pages 210, 218–220). Here, too, you have results instantly at hand. But the great advantage of the photostat process over the contact copier is that you are not limited to a 1:1 scale; with the aid of the stat camera, you can enlarge and reduce.

Copyproof Materials

The following materials are used in the Copyproof process:

1. Negative material CPN used with the positive material CPP produces paper prints for black-and-white line art.
2. Negative material CPN used with the positive material CPF produces transparent film prints for black-and-white line art.
3. Negative material CPTN used with the positive material CPP and the film CPF produces continuous tone (half-tone) prints on paper and film.

4. Negative material CPRV used with the positive material CPP or with CPF produces reversals of black into white, and white into black line art.
5. Developer (Activator) CP 296B is for CPN and CPTN Developer CP 298B is for CPN and CPRV.
6. Processor Copyproof CP 38 accommodates materials up to 14".

These materials are available only in black and white. You cannot produce color prints with them.

The positive materials CPP and CPF also come with adhesive backs. For most uses the sizes 8¼" x 11⅝" and 12¼" x 16⅞" are altogether adequate.

Setting the Exposure Time

Determine what the exposure times are for the different Copyproof materials, and set your camera accordingly. All the information given here applies to the materials now available for use in the Repromaster 2001 camera shown on page 246. (Exposure times vary with reduction and enlargement, fine line art, or large areas of black, and so on, depending on the nature of the art and the result desired.) With both lenses that can be used in this camera, the basic exposure time is 18 seconds with an aperture setting of 22 for a 100% reproduction (1:1). (This aperture setting is the one normally used because it provides a sharp image.) When programmed for this basic exposure time, the camera will automatically recalculate to the corresponding exposure time if you change the aperture or the scale of enlargement or reduction.

Shorter exposure times produce heavier lines. The intensified light of longer exposure times fills in and makes lines thinner or produces breaks in them. If you want to make a radical reduction of a line drawing, it is

therefore advisable to lower the basic exposure time to about 10 seconds so that thin lines still reproduce. By changing exposure times, you can vary the thickness of lines, as the illustrations on pages 224–27 show.

The copyboard of the camera has a piece of cardboard on it that is white on one side and black on the other. With originals that have very fine lines in them, use the black side to reduce the possibility of glare and reflective background causing overexposure and gaps in the lines. If you want to make lines thinner, use the white side and increase the exposure time.

Average Exposure Times for Negative Materials

The following are for a reproduction scale of 1:1 (100%):

CPN line material	Aperture 22	18 seconds
CPTN halftone material	Aperture 22	6 seconds
CPRV reverse material	Aperture 22	54 seconds

With the reverse material CPRV that is used to retain white—that is, negative—lettering or drawings on a black background, you should, with an aperture setting of 22, reduce the exposure time to 40 seconds if the lines are thin. Because enlargements with this material require unusually long exposure times, you can compensate somewhat by reducing the aperture to 16. This widens the aperture, letting more light in and subsequently shortening the exposure time.

For extreme reductions, which call for very short exposure times, an aperture opening of 32 or 45 will allow you a wide enough range of exposure times to experiment with the weight of lines or copy (as in making lines thicker and thinner).

Calculating Enlargements and Reductions

Because the camera measures the sizes of images in percentages, the only rational way to determine the sizes of enlargements or reductions is with a pocket calculator or a proportion scale. For example, an original that is 8″ wide is to be enlarged to 20″:

20 ÷ 8 and press the percent key = 250%

For a reduction, do just the reverse. If a width of 20″ is to be reduced to 8″, then the arithmetic looks like this:

8 ÷ 20 and press the percent key = 40%

Since the automatic electronic system in the camera gives an exposure time of 8 seconds (100% = 18 seconds) for 40% with an aperture setting of 22, you may wind up with lines thinner than you want. In that case, take 15 seconds as your basic (100%) exposure time. This will give you a new exposure time of 7 seconds. If that is still too much, take 13 seconds as your base and use a 6-second exposure.

A change in the basic exposure time can be made independent of the enlargement or reduction setting you have just made, depending on the desired result and your experience with similar artwork. The camera will automatically calculate the new values. If it should happen that with a reduction the percentage falls under 25% (the 150 mm lens of this camera reduces only between 50–25%), then you will have to make an interim print. For example, an original that is 30″ wide is to be reduced to 4″ or 13.33%. Set the camera for 25% (the smallest possible reduction). This will give you an interim print 7½″ wide, which you can then reduce to 4″.

30 x 25 and press percent key = 75% or 7½″
4 ÷ 7½ and press the percent key = 53.33%

For enlargements over 400% (the largest possible enlargement), you proceed in the same way, making one or more interim prints as required.

239

If you have a large number of originals of various sizes to reproduce, then calculate the percentages in advance and sort out your originals in a rising or descending order. For example, 67%, 72%, 94%, 112%, 154%, 230%, and so on, so that you can avoid endlessly cranking your machine up and down.

The Procedure

During the camera adjustment the matte film, also equipped with format sizes, is aligned with the formats inscribed on the cardboard below with the machine set at 100%. The matte film is then fastened along the hinged side of the cover with a strip of tape. This matte film serves as an edge alignment for the negative material and should *not be moved anymore*.

Center the original on the format cardboard. Enter the exposure time. Use the left-hand crank to set the proper percentage number; use the right-hand one to focus the camera.

Now, working under a red light, center the negative material under the matte film with the coated side down. Turn on the vacuum and expose the material. After exposure, *slowly* push the negative and positive papers, coated sides facing each other, into their respective slots in the processor. If you push the papers too quickly, black areas may appear on the edge of the positive paper. The 2 rollers inside press the papers together. Paper can be separated from the negative after 30 seconds; film, after 60.

With the halftone material CPTN, the time you allow for developing to take place can vary from 15 to 60 seconds, depending on the shading you want. Short contact times will produce soft tones; longer times, harder ones. With this material, you always have to use fresh developer.

240

Throw the negative away. The positive of the CPP or CPF material will show a thick, heavy black. Even the finest lines will stand out sharply on the white background. The positive, whether paper or film, must in any case either be watered down or held under running water, or at least thoroughly rinsed off, because unwashed positives will turn brown with time. A print dryer is not necessary. You can hang the wet positive up and let most of the water drip off. Then, on a glass plate or on the camera cover, use a squeegee to blot the moisture out of it and hang it up again to dry thoroughly (or you can finish the drying process with a hair dryer). Because these papers have a synthetic base, they dry very quickly and can be worked with again almost immediately.

The developer will turn dark brown very quickly. For line work, this has no adverse effect. The developer can be reconditioned by mixing it 50:50 with fresh developer.

The material can be retouched with an X-Acto knife or with pens available in art stores under the name Silver Genie. One pencil bleaches out black; the other fixes the change.

The Copyproof process is useful for all occasions when you need to enlarge or reduce drawings, lettering, photos, and so on, and when you want copies that you can use right away. The entire process including calculating the scale, setting the camera, exposure, and developing cannot take more than 5 minutes per copy.

The prerequisite for this kind of speed and results is, of course, a high-quality reprocamera. Such a camera has a vertical optical axis and takes up relatively little space as compared to a Lucy. It can also be used to make drawings, tracings, and graphic translations, as can a Lucy. If you do not have one of these machines yourself, printing shops listed in the yellow pages of the telephone book will do copy work on Copyproof materials for you.

The Copycolor Process

Although the Copyproof process can produce only black-and-white prints, it is possible now, with the Copycolor process, to produce color prints on paper or film by way of a paper negative. This process works in basically the same way as Copyproof does. The material is exposed on the reprocamera, and the negative and positive are then run through the processer.

However, you *cannot* use these materials in red light. You need a special dark-room light that emits a yellowish green light. You have to put tape over the illuminated red switches on the reprocamera because the negative material is sensitive to even that much red light. The negative material also has to be kept in a refrigerator at approximately 44° F. (7° C). Then, too, there are films especially developed to control contrasts in this process as well as a set of filters in the 3 basic colors—yellow, cyan blue, and magenta. These come in 6 different density shades and are inserted in the filter holder according to the instructions on the package.

Copycolor Materials

The following materials are used in the Copycolor process.

1. The negative material CCN used with the positive material CCP, a paper coated on both sides, produces *matte* prints.
2. The negative material CCN used with the positive material CCG, a paper coated on both sides, produces either *matte* or *glossy* prints.
3. The negative material CCN used with the positive mate-

rial CCF produces prints on transparent film .10 mm
thick. This film can be used for slides or overhead projector material.
4.   Developer (Activator) CC292 B.
5.   Contrast Control Films as follows:
     CC1 for reproducing line originals.
     CC2 for reproducing line and halftone originals.
     CC3 for reproducing slide originals.
6.   Filter set in yellow, cyan blue, and magenta in 6 differ-
     ent density shades.
7.   Special dark-room light.

If you take into account the storage of the negative
materials in an extra refrigerator, the acquisition of the
dark-room light, the contrast control films, the filters,
and the somewhat expensive materials, then the Copy-

color process is financially viable only if you do a great deal of work in color reproduction. If you need such prints now and then, it is cheaper to have them made for you in a copy shop. However, do not confuse these Copycolor prints with normal color photocopies, which are made on a color copying machine. In addition to Copycolor, color prints can be made with Cibachrome, and Kodak Ektaflex PCT processes.

Coloring Copyproof Materials

The Artservice Colorsystem makes it possible to use a Copyproof print to convert a black-and-white line original to one or more colors. To do this, you need the following materials: The reversal material CPRV (to make the negative), the positive paper CPG (smooth, with a glossy surface), the developer CP 298B, the bleaching chemicals A and B (manufactured under the name Chamtech), a chamois cloth, Q-Tips or cotton pads, and water-soluble Dr. Martin dyes (synchromatic transparent water dyes). The essential factor for flawless results is always to use *fresh* Copyproof activator (developer). Here's the procedure:

1. Lay the CPG positive in a bleach bath made of 50:50 parts A and B of a developer. Mix just as much as you will need immediately, because the mixture remains usable for only 3 to 7 days. Then, too, the top of the bottle in which it is stored cannot be screwed on tight because the mixture produces gases that will explode a sealed container.
2. After 30 seconds, the black picture will disappear. Rinse the print in water and dry it. The black picture now appears in *pure white* on a pale yellowish background.

3. Fasten the upper edge of the print to the glass plate with a strip of Scotch tape.

4. Soften a chamois cloth in clean water and then wring it out until it is almost dry.

5. Moisten a cotton pad with a little of Dr. Martin's dye. Starting at the top, rub the ink vigorously into the areas you want to color until it is evenly applied. The important thing is to have the ink thoroughly rubbed into the areas that will later carry the color. If you are dealing only with small areas or with lines, you can use Q-Tips (cotton swabs) or a brush to color them in.

6. Fold the chamois cloth twice and roll it into a cylinder. Then, starting at the top of your work, pull this down to the bottom to wipe away the excess ink.

This procedure requires practice because some excess ink is always left on white areas and then has to be dabbed or wiped off with the chamois. It can happen that you will have to repeat the coloring and wiping operations several times, because repeated wiping can leave the color too pale.

If the color has become too intense, you can continue wiping with the chamois until you reach the lightness you want. The print can be rinsed, which will also make the color paler. With water, however, you do not have the same control over the degree of paleness as you do with the wiping process.

If you cannot or do not want to use reversal material CPRV, make a print on CPG, using CPN as your negative and the usual CP 296B activator as your developer. Here's how:

1. After rinsing and drying, lay the CPG positive in the bleach bath, remove it once the black has disappeared, rinse the print, and dry it.

2. Moisten a cotton pad with Litho red (a dye), with which the negative material reacts as it does with black. Rub the Litho red into the print and then wipe it (as described in steps 5 and 6 earlier).

3.   This sheet, which is now the reverse of the original, is shot again in the camera and transferred to CPN and developed with CPG. After the bleach bath and drying, it can be colored with any color you choose and then wiped off.

This procedure saves your changing the activator and also avoids the long exposure times needed with the CPRV material. The disadvantages are that you have to use 2 more sheets of Copyproof and have an additional step in the procedure. You will have to weigh the advantages and disadvantages for yourself in each particular situation.

Reprocamera

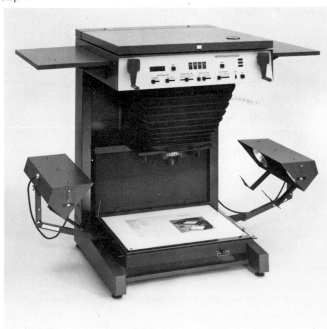

The ColorKey Process

In 4-color offset printing, a black-and-white film negative is made for each of the 4 printing colors—yellow, magenta (red), cyan (blue), and black. And from these negatives, 4 printing plates are made. The finished 4-color print is produced by printing the 4 colors one over the other with the 4 plates. However, to make corrections possible before the plates are made and so as to save a great deal of time and expense, 3M developed the ColorKey process. Light-sensitive films in the 4 basic colors are exposed in combination with the 4 negatives. When they are developed, they can be laid one on top of another on a light table, and in this combined form they give an impression of what the finished print will look like. Today, these films are used primarily as graphic design materials. Because the film is exposed in a contact process, the negative has to be the same size as the print will be.

ColorKey overlays 8.4

ColorKey does not produce halftones. It is purely a line process, and to get a film positive, you need a line negative (which can also be screened to create an impression of halftones). Only the 4 basic colors are produced with a *film positive;* all other colors are produced with a *film negative.* There are transparent standard tones, the number of which has been expanded by the Pantone system; and if we consider all the transparent tones now available in one form or another, we see that a vast range of colors can be produced with a variety of combinations. In addition there are opaque colors, however they do not cover completely. I do not recommend these rather unattractive opaque colors, and I would suggest using Chromatec or Letrachrome Dry Transfer instead. All you need is a source of ultraviolet light and a plate of glass. There are ultraviolet exposure units on the market usable for ColorKey, Chromatec, and Letrachrome, but this is a matter of money and how often one actually works with those processes. Here again I would recommend buying a unit with a vacuum pump. (See also the section on Letrachrome, page 251.)

The Procedure

The workroom does not have to be excessively dark, however you should not use any strong ultraviolet room light. Lay the individual elements on top of each other as shown in the illustration on the right. The glass should be free of bubbles; be sure to use black paper to prevent glare. A photo lamp or an ultraviolet bulb clamped to a support will serve as a source of light. At a distance of about 16″ (40 cm), the exposure time for transparent ColorKey is about 2¾ minutes. You can determine the exact exposure time required for your particular light source and distance of light from the material by using a Stouffer gray scale (available in art supply shops).

After exposing the ColorKey material, lay it coated side up on the plate of glass and pour some ColorKey developer over it. Using gauze or wad of cotton, rub the coated side of the ColorKey material with *light* circular motions until the drawing appears. The parts not covered by the black areas of the negative will be hardened by the ultraviolet light. The unhardened areas will be washed off by the developer. Once all the subtle details of the drawing are visible, rinse the drawing under running water and dry it with a paper towel. Unlike photographic film, ColorKey does not have any gelatin in its coating, so once the drops of water are wiped off, it is dry and immediately ready for further use. The following brands of felt-tipped markers can be used, in any color you like, to color over ColorKey Opaque White, and the white will not show through at all: Mars Graphic 3000 (60 colors), Stabilo Pen 68 (50 colors), and Stabilo Layout (70 colors). Color over the coated side of the film with the marker. When the film is dry, just rub the film off to remove the marker traces outside the coating.

Making a Negative

If you do not have a line negative, use orange (transparent) ColorKey and the process just described above to make a negative from a film positive. Put the finished negative on a light table and examine it for flaws (spots, holes, and so on). Small flaws can be repaired with Film Opaque Brush-On Ink, and larger flaws can be covered with (self-adhering) masking film. This orange-colored and *transparent* negative can be placed over other ColorKey negatives or positives to check that everything is properly aligned during complex procedures. This capability is what makes ColorKey orange superior in such instances to a normal, nontransparent negative. Its disadvantage is its cost, for ColorKey orange costs as much as any of the other ColorKey colors.

A cheaper way of achieving the same ends is to use normal line film (such as Kodalith or Fuji-Litho film) that you can expose by the contact method or in a stat camera. Then, instead of processing it with film developer, use Ilfo-Speed Paper Developer (60 seconds) and Ilfo-Speed Paper Fixative Bath (30 seconds). Dry the wet film with a hair dryer and you have, for a very small investment of time, a negative that you can then use in ColorKey, Letrachrome, and Chromatec procedures. There is also a fluid called a "transparentizer" which renders photostat paper (matte or glossy, not DP) translucent for sharper and faster exposure with ColorKey.

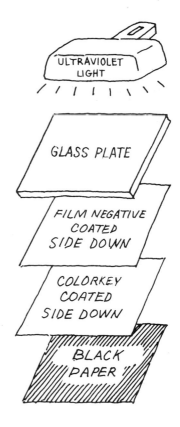

ULTRAVIOLET LIGHT

GLASS PLATE

FILM NEGATIVE COATED SIDE DOWN

COLORKEY COATED SIDE DOWN

BLACK PAPER

1

2

3

4

5

The original was made up of several black-and-white photographs, which, for compositional reasons, were mounted together. From this montage, high-contrast prints (color separations, that is, halftone separations because they were black and white) were made using different exposure times. From these paper prints, negative films were made, which were then used in turn to expose the different ColorKey films needed. Finally, a montage of those ColorKey films over each other produced the finished draft for this postage stamp.

A total of 5 ColorKey films were needed: The sky (Fig. 1), the first stage (Fig. 2), and the second stage (not pictured) all used the same blue. The second stage was then produced in magenta as well. Combined with cyan, this yielded the violet shown in Fig. 3. Finally, the black of Fig. 4 was added to give depth. A strip of yellow film mounted under the blue (Fig. 5) added the green of the grass.

Presenting ColorKey Overlays

Since ColorKey overlays, because of their transparency and brilliant color, are ideal for viewing on a light table or against a light source, they should be mounted like photographic slides.

Cut out double mats and tape a piece of tracing paper or matte acetate or vellum paper over the bottom so that you can view the layered overlays against the light. Since most projects involve several colors, it is a good idea to put register marks on each negative so that it will be easier to line up the positives later.

Two strips of Scotch tape are adequate for mounting the individual overlays. Then it is easy to replace some overlays with others later if necessary.

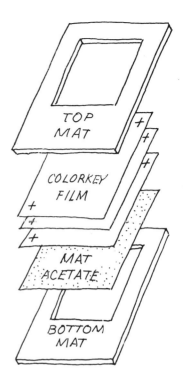

Making Letrachrome Prints

Letrachrome prints are turned out one at a time. In this direct imaging process, ultraviolet-sensitive inks, together with line film negatives or screen negatives are exposed to ultraviolet light. When layered together or overprinted later, these items create the impression of a finished print.

The Letrachrome Direct Imaging Process is used primarily in doing color work for presentations that will be of near-print quality. With this process, you can make prints on white plastic paper or transparencies on clear acetate. On both materials you can apply innumerable layers of color on top of or next to each other. The layers of ink are so thin that the finished product really looks as if it were printed.

251

One great advantage of this process is that only tap water is needed for developing. Three kits are supplied, with the following:

1. Plastic paper, inks, Color Product Selector (Pantone), humidity gauge, exposure calculator, squeegee, coating bars in their quiverlike storage tubes, color mixing tubes, pipettes, cleaner/etch solution, exposure test set, formula and exposure guide, Liquid Gloss, and corrector fluid.
2. Work area for applying ink layers (coating unit), with glass plate and roll of paper, developing tray, spray nozzle, and pipettes. An area that can handle formats of 14″ x 20″ (35 x 50 cm) is altogether adequate because one hardly ever uses formats larger than that.
3. Ultraviolet exposure unit with flourescent tubes and vacuum (for screen work) or without vacuum, plus ultraviolet spotlight. Letrachrome offers the Econolite exposure unit for formats of 8¼″ x 12″ and 12″ x 16½″ (DIN a 4 and DIN a 3). For most work—and especially for the Dry Transfer Process—these formats are fully adequate.

The Direct Imaging Process

Before you begin processing, determine the basic exposure time of the ultraviolet exposure unit or light source that you are using. Make a rough test as follows.

Preliminary Test
Lay a narrow strip of plastic paper on your working surface, put a drop of Pantone Process Blue on the paper, and use a No. 1 metal bar to roll the drop out into a strip about 4″ (10 cm) long. Dry the strip with a hair dryer.

Cover ⅔ of the strip with a piece of black paper or masking film, and expose it to ultraviolet light for 30 seconds. Now pull your covering paper back another third so that $^2/_3$ of the strip can now be exposed for another 30 seconds. Remove the cover altogether, and expose the entire strip for a final 30 seconds. Put the paper on a glass plate, and rinse it in cold water, ideally with the spray nozzle. Wipe it off with a cleaning swab, squeegee it, and dry it with the hair dryer. If, for example, $^2/_3$ of the strip remains while the rest was washed off, then the *approximate* exposure time is 2 x 30 = 60 seconds.

Exact Exposure Test

Because the result of 60 seconds is only an approximation, use 5-second intervals to determine the *exact* exposure time.

Cover a larger piece of plastic paper ($6^3/_4$" x $8^3/_4$" [17 x 22 cm]) with the same Pantone Process Blue. When you are using the very thin Pantone inks in the Direct Imaging process, use the application bar as follows:

Dry the bar carefully with a lint-free cloth. Hold the bar firmly with your fingertips, and draw it toward you *without letting it turn*—that is, use it as a squeegee. Using light pressure, pull the bar along at a uniform rate of speed. Depending on the width of the paper, use you left hand on the first third of the sheet from the left, your right on the second third.

Draw the excess ink off the sheet and onto the paper underlayer on your working surface. Put the bar back into its tube. It is best to dry the ink immediately with the hair dryer because lint can settle on the wet ink very quickly.

Fasten the manufacturer's exposure test negative *right side up* to the plastic paper with a piece of tape, and expose it for 45 seconds. Now cover Field 1 with masking film, and expose for 5 seconds more. Next, cover Fields 1 and 2, and expose for another 5 seconds. Then cover Fields 1, 2, and 3, and expose for 5 more seconds. Lastly, cover Fields 1 to 4, and expose for a final 5 seconds.

After rinsing and drying, you will have a print in which the stars of the test sheet in the upper and lower rows will be, in varying degrees, underexposed, overexposed, or correct. The test figure has a circle in the middle of it. In the upper row, this circle should be clearly defined, and the first row of rays around the circle should be neither underexposed nor overexposed. The same applies for the lower, negative row.

Because, in our example, the best results fall in Field 3, we conclude that the *basic* exposure time for the exposure unit we are using is 55 seconds, provided that the color is *Process Blue* (as Factor 1) and that the same humidity prevails as did during the test. Read the percentage of humidity from the humidity gauge, and enter it onto the test sheet with an indelible felt marker. Let's assume it was 75% in our test. From these 2 values (factor and time), you can now calculate—or more exactly, read off—the exposure times for all other colors, always taking into account, of course, the prevailing humidity.

Using the Calculation Tables
Don't let the mention of exposure calculators and the formula and exposure guide with all its tables throw you for a loop. These things all sound much more complicated than they are, and once you have worked with them a few times, you won't have the least bit of trouble. Here are some examples to show what I mean.

If the humidity remains 75%, as in the example above, then set the exposure calculator on page B to the basic exposure time of 55. The numbers in the stamped-out field represent *seconds*. The numbers in the row to the left (except for 0.8 and 1) are extension factors. These factors are also found in the yellow (butt register) and blue (overprint) columns of the formula and exposure guide. Because the bar used most often is No. 3, use only the *middle vertical* column.

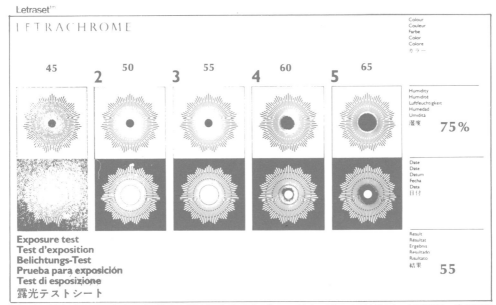

Letraset™

LETRACHROME

	Colour
	Couleur
	Farbe
	Color
	Colore
	カラー

45   2   50   3   55   4   60   5   65

Humidity
Humidité
Luftfeuchtigkeit
Humedad
Umidità
湿度   75%

Date
Date
Datum
Fecha
Data
日付

Exposure test
Test d'exposition
Belichtungs-Test
Prueba para exposición
Test di esposizione
露光テストシート

Result
Résultat
Ergebnis
Resultado
Risultato
結果   55

Letraset and Letrachrome are trademarks of Letraset Ltd, Esselte Pentaflex Corp and Letraset Canada Ltd, © Letraset Ltd 1984   ⊗ ESSELTE

Let's assume we want to make a draft utilizing 3 different tones of brown. We look up the inks we want in the Pantone Color Product Selector, and from the formula and exposure guide we take the factor that applies to each color.

If we want to apply the colors *next to* each other, we use the yellow column (butt register). If we want the colors *on top of* each other, we use the blue column (overprint). Because the colors are transparent, overprinting will create mixed colors.

All the formulas in this book assume use of the wire coating bar No. 3, which is the bar used most often. If we want the color to look lighter, we apply a thinner layer of ink, using the No. 0 bar. If we are working with acetate, we use the No. 5 wire bar.

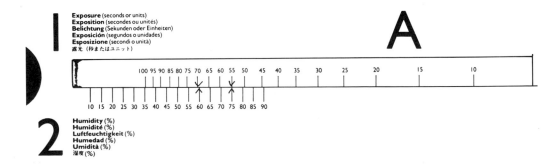

FACTOR	TIME
	55 — ◀ Basic exposure
0.8	44
1.0	55
1.2	66
1.4	77
1.6	88
1.8	99
2.0	110
2.2	121
2.4	132
2.6	143
2.8	154
3.0	165
3.2	176
3.4	187
3.6	198
3.8	209
4.0	220
4.2	231
4.4	242
4.6	253
4.8	264
5.0	275
5.2	286
5.4	297
5.6	308
5.8	319
6.0	330
6.2	341
6.4	352
6.6	363
6.8	374
7.0	385
7.2	396
7.4	407
7.6	418
7.8	429
8.0	440
8.2	451
8.4	462
8.6	473
8.8	484
9.0	495
9.2	506
9.4	517
9.6	528
9.8	539
10.0	550

Set the top figure to the basic exposure (adjusted exposure test result from side A).

The correct exposure for every exposure factor up to 10 is shown inside the window. For factors over 10, refer to half the desired factor and double the result.

For more information, see the Letrachrome User Manual.

Colors Next to Each Other (Butt Register)/Bar No. 3

Ink 467 U	Factor 1.2	Time 80 sec*
Ink 464 U	Factor 3.4	Time 187 sec
Ink 462 U	Factor 3.8	Time 209 sec

Colors on Top of Each Other (Overprint)/Bar No. 3

Ink 467 U	Factor 1.2	Time 80 sec*
Ink 464 U	Factor 8.4	Time 462 sec
Ink 462 U	Factor 9.4	Time 517 sec

*Experience has shown that the first color application can be burnt in more intensively. We therefore add about 20% to the exposure time given in the index; that is, 66 seconds + 14 seconds = 80 seconds.

Changes in Humidity

If the humidity drops, which generally happens in the winter in heated rooms without humidifiers, we have to use different exposure times.

If the humidity drops to 60%, for instance, go to page A of the exposure calculator and set the basic exposure time of 55 seconds (which will always apply whenever you use this particular source of light) at the humidity prevailing when you made your original exposure test—that is, 75%.

Above the humidity value of 60%, the new basic exposure time is 70 seconds. Turn the calculator over, and on Page B, push "70" into the window. This column now contains all the applicable exposure times.

Exposure (seconds or units)
Exposition (secondes ou unités)
Belichtung (Sekunden oder Einheiten)
Exposición (segundos o unidades)
Esposizione (secondi o unità)
露光 (秒またはユニット)

Humidity (%)
Humidité (%)
Luftfeuchtigkeit (%)
Humedad (%)
Umidità (%)
湿度 (%)

If you continue working with the same colors as earlier, you find the following changes in the exposure times for colors *next to* each other (butt register):

Ink 467 U	Factor 1.2	Time 100 sec*
Ink 464 U	Factor 3.4	Time 238 sec
Ink 462 U	Factor 3.8	Time 266 sec

And we will also have different times for colors *on top of* each other (overprint):

Ink 167 U	Factor 1.2	Time 100 sec*
Ink 464 U	Factor 8.4	Time 588 sec
Ink 462 U	Factor 9.4	Time 658 sec

*84 seconds + 16 seconds = 100 seconds.

Mixing Colors

With the help of the color-mixing table *(formula and exposure guide)* you can produce 488 tones on the Pantone scale from the basic colors. The advantage of this scale is that the color numbers of Letrachrome correspond to those of other Pantone products, such as printing inks, felt-tipped markers, and colored papers. And this is true all over the world. In other words, a draft can be reprinted anywhere with exactly the same colors. If the printer has the color numbers used in the original, he can mix precisely the right color printing ink.

The color "Superblack" is a new product that requires a markedly shorter exposure time than the 2 other blacks—black and Ultrablack—and is also even blacker. There is also now an opaque white. Because all the other colors in the Letrachrome system are transparent and produce mixed tones when superimposed on each other, opaque colors can now be produced with the aid of the opaque white. Under the color that is to be made opaque, expose and develop a layer of white with the same negative. White lines, lettering, or shapes can, of course, also be produced with the opaque white.

A transparent liquid called Clear Extender is used to thin the colors. To produce progressions in airbrush

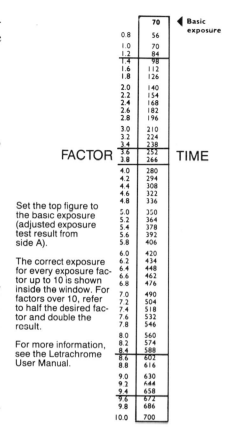

FACTOR — TIME

70 ◀ Basic exposure

FACTOR	TIME
0.8	56
1.0	70
1.2	84
1.4	98
1.6	112
1.8	126
2.0	140
2.2	154
2.4	168
2.6	182
2.8	196
3.0	210
3.2	224
3.4	238
3.6	252
3.8	266
4.0	280
4.2	294
4.4	308
4.6	322
4.8	336
5.0	350
5.2	364
5.4	378
5.6	392
5.8	406
6.0	420
6.2	434
6.4	448
6.6	462
6.8	476
7.0	490
7.2	504
7.4	518
7.6	532
7.8	546
8.0	560
8.2	574
8.4	588
8.6	602
8.8	616
9.0	630
9.2	644
9.4	658
9.6	672
9.8	686
10.0	700

Set the top figure to the basic exposure (adjusted exposure test result from side A).

The correct exposure for every exposure factor up to 10 is shown inside the window. For factors over 10, refer to half the desired factor and double the result.

For more information, see the Letrachrome User Manual.

applications, thin the ink with tap water. Here, however, you should note that the factors in the exposure tables that you normally use in mixing colors no longer apply. It is therefore a good idea to conduct some exposure tests beforehand.

The inks are mixed drop by drop because they can be used very sparingly. From the "color fan" you take the desired color number, which, in Column A of the formula and exposure guide, gives the most exact mixture. If the color needs to be only an approximation, then the data in Column B will suffice. Column C indicates the amount needed to color a sheet of plastic paper 8" x 14¼" with a No. 3 bar.

The 60-mL bottles of ink are equipped with droppers. Count the prescribed number of drops into an empty mixing bottle and mix carefully by repeatedly drawing the liquid up in a plastic pipette or by gently rocking the bottle back and forth. Do not shake the bottle vigorously, or you will produce air bubbles.

Often you will not use up all the ink you have mixed. Write the color number on a label and stick the label on the bottle; the ink is too valuable to throw away.

The inks can be stored for a year, which is to say that within this period, the exposure factors in the formula and exposure guide still apply. Between one year and a year and a half, the exposure times will have to be extended. After a year and a half, the colors are no longer useable.

Application and Developing

Using a coating bar, distribute the ink evenly over the plastic paper, then dry it *immediately* with a hair dryer. The color may show spots or stripes at this point. It is a good idea to use a larger paper than the finished format because this gives you an opportunity to place the negative in an optimal position where the spots will disappear under the black forms of the negative (and can later be rinsed away). But if the color application is simply too poor, wash the entire color area off with the spray nozzle. Before exposure, the color is water soluble.

Fasten the negative onto the colored and dried sheet of plastic paper with 2 strips of tape to keep the negative from slipping. Be sure, too, that the negative is placed with the *proper side up* (right-reading side).

If you are working with complicated layerings of color over each other or side by side or with 4-color process screens, then you will have to work very exactly and provide all the negatives you use with register marks. The process can work so precisely that you can use film negatives with a 60% (120-line) screen to simulate, for example, a 4-color print as a "proof."

After exposure, slightly dampen the glass plate in your sink, lay your paper on it, press down a little on the paper so that it will not slip, then spray it evenly with the spray nozzle. Carefully wipe the surface with a wad of cotton. The layers are particularly sensitive when you are laying one color over another. Rinse again, and repeat this process until the positive form comes up clean. Now squeegee the paper, dry it with a hair dryer, apply the next color immediately, and continue in this fashion until you have completed all your planned steps.

To simplify your task and guarantee that it goes off smoothly, mix all the colors you will need in advance, label the bottles with the mixture numbers, and establish the order in which the colors will be applied (and therefore the order in which you will execute the different steps in your work). Note all the steps, together with the exposure times for each color, for in this process the combination of colors you are creating exists only in your own mind (which makes this work a thrilling adventure sometimes).

If, for example, you have already applied 3 colors,

you will not be able to judge how the fourth will look in combination with them until you have put it on and exposed it. Errors cannot be corrected at this stage, and for that reason you may have to repeat all your steps, replacing the color that did not work with a new mixture.

Making Transfers

You can buy ready-made transfer materials (Letraset and Chartpac) with which you can apply lettering, symbols, screens, etc., by transferring the adhesive-backed material onto various surfaces. There are also 2 systems (Letrachrome and Chromatec) that allow you to make your own rub-down transfer material.

The Source of Light
These 2 systems, like ColorKey, make use of a chemical layer that solidifies when it is exposed to light. This means that an ultraviolet light is shone through a film negative onto a photosensitive surface. The areas not covered by the blackened parts of the negative solidify. These areas cannot then be washed away later by the developer (or by water, depending on the process).

The lamp used has to be high in ultraviolet light. You can use an ordinary 300-watt sunlamp, a halogen film bulb (a small quartz lamp that throws out a tremendous amount of light), or exposure units especially designed for such uses. These units are available from a number of manufacturers. They include a timer and, in some models, a vacuum pump. The light source is an ultraviolet fluorescent lamp. Your task will of course be easier if you have a unit in which the distance between the light source and the material to be exposed is always the same; and if the unit presses the film material firmly together; and if you know what exposure times to use with it to achieve the desired results. Your decision on what kind of light source to choose will depend both on how much you want to spend and on how frequently you will want to or have to use procedures requiring its use. See, too, the ultraviolet exposure units for Letrachrome Direct Imaging (page 252).

The Letrachrome Dry Transfer Process

This process, like the previously described Direct Imaging System, has the invaluable advantage that the developing is done with water alone.

The Process
The base material or carrier material is an acetate that has a matte side and a glossy side. Lay the material on the working area with the glossy side up, and apply a *preliminary coating* with a No. 8 roller. Dry this coating with a hair dryer. In this system, the consistency of the liquid materials (preliminary coating and inks) is much thicker; they are therefore applied with rollers different from those used in the Direct Imaging process. Here, too, however, the rollers are held at *both ends* (see Application of the Ink, page 258). It is a good idea to put some household cleaner (Mister Clean, Ajax, etc.) in the water for the roller holders or tubes. The cleaner helps cut the excess ink.

Because the inks are very thick, you have to keep shaking the bottles until you hear the ball rattling inside. Now you can apply the color you want with a No. 20 roller and dry it with a hair dryer. This takes longer than with the Direct Imaging process.

Next, put the dry, coated sheet into the exposure unit with the *coated side down*—that is, away from the source of light. If the ink is not entirely dry, you can prevent it from sticking to the exposure unit by laying a sheet of polyester film underneath. Place the negative with the *right-reading side up* on the Dry Transfer sheet and expose it. All colors take the same exposure time, which is considerably shorter than with Direct Imaging and is usually somewhere between 10 and 20 seconds, depending on your exposure unit. For your specific light source, you have to test for the correct exposure time.

After exposure, lay the sheet in a tray filled with tap water for 1 minute. The image will appear in that time. Rinse the sheet, using *only* the spray nozzle, until the positive sections come up clear. Once the sheet has been dried with the hair dryer, it is ready to be used.

In this system there are 12 opaque colors. To mix the 488 colors of the Pantone Color Selector, however, you need only the 9 basic colors. The mixing proportions are contained in a separate formula book, but the Pantone Color Selector is the same as for Direct Imaging.

Mixing Dry Transfer Colors
The formula book tells you the amounts of ink to use. Attach a plastic measuring tube to the ink bottle and then squeeze into the tube the amount of ink called for in the book. Then squeeze the contents of the tube into a transparent plastic bag. Follow the same procedure with the other colors needed for your mixture, then mix the inks together by rolling them in the plastic bag with an L-shaped metal instrument. Cut off the tip of the plastic bag, and squeeze a strip of the mixture out onto the pre-coated sheet the way you squeeze toothpaste out of a tube and roll it on.

If you use the same color mixtures often, make up large quantities and save them in labeled bottles.

Advantages of the Two Letrachrome Processes
Colors in the Direct Imaging system that are exposed according to the exposure table for colors *next to* each

other will stick only if applied *next to* each other and not *on top of* each other. In practice, this has the following consequences:

If you want to put, for example, yellow lettering on a light blue background, you will need only 1 negative (one with the lettering on it). The yellow ink is applied, dried, and then exposed together with the negative. After the rinsing, the yellow lettering appears in positive form on the blank background. Now apply the blue ink to the entire surface of this dry sheet and expose it *without the negative.* For both exposures use the factor for colors lying next to each other (butt register). In rinsing, the blue washes off from the yellow lettering, and the blue background borders perfectly on it, without being the least bit out of register.

If you repeat the entire process, this time however using the factor for colors *on top of* (overprint) each other for the blue ink, the mixing of yellow and blue will give you green lettering on a blue background. So we see that longer exposure times change the adhesiveness of the Direct Imaging inks. Depending on the particular requirements of your draft, you will have to use one method or the other, or possibly mix the two.

In using the Dry Transfer system, you use the values for colors *next to* each other. Because these inks are opaque, putting one color on top of another on a single sheet would not produce any usable results. For example, you want to make a monogram draft into a one-piece rub-down transfer element with the letters A (yellow), M (red), and O (blue) on a black background. You proceed as follows. You need only one negative with the letters on it. Apply yellow to the pre-coated transfer sheet and, once the coating is dry, place the negative on the sheet. Cover the letters *M* and *O* with masking film or black paper, and expose the negative and sheet.

After washing and drying the sheet, coat it with red, and place the negative in the proper position (that is, so that the yellow *A* lies directly under the *A* in the negative). Now cover the *O*. After exposure, washing, and drying, apply blue, place the negative in the right position again, and expose. After developing and drying this stage, apply the last color—black—to the whole sheet. Use carefully cut strips of masking film to cover everything but the rectangular field of the monogram. After exposure and washing, you will then have—in the form of a complete transfer symbol—the letters *A M O* in 3 different colors on a black background.

The Chromatec Process

In the Chromatec process, the first thing to do is coat a Chromaslick sheet. In addition to the necessary inks and chemicals, you need a level working surface with a roll of newsprint nearby. The newsprint is used to soak up excess chemicals and to cover the work surface. The paper can be torn off when dirty and replaced with fresh, clean paper. You'll also need a long metal clamp to hold the Chromaslick sheet in place.

You will need 3 rollers, called coating bars. These are steel bars that are wound with a silver wire and that are kept standing on end in a kind of quiver. There is an individual tube for each bar, and each tube is filled with a special solvent. The inks are sold under the label Coates 50/50 Color System. They are available in 22 standard colors, which are always mixed in the proportion 1:1 to produce 350 different color tones. They come in plastic squeeze bottles. Other necessary materials are noted in the description of the process.

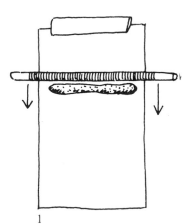

The Process
Chromaslick sheets are not the same on both sides. You can use Scotch tape to find out which is the working side; the tape will not stick to the right side. Clamp the sheet to your working surface with this side up, and begin as follows.

1. Application of the Ink With the squeeze bottle, apply a strip of standard or mixed ink across the Chromaslick sheet about 2″ (5 cm) from the top. Then using an ink roller almost as you would a squeegee—that is, without letting the roller turn—draw it from the top of the sheet to the bottom, spreading the ink evenly. This requires a fine touch and considerable practice. If the ink layer comes out uneven, you can smooth it by slightly turning the roller while drawing. But the rule is to apply the ink with one stroke of the roller. Then the ink coating should be dried immediately with a hair dryer to prevent lint from settling on the wet ink. If you want a *transparent* transfer material, as for color film for an overhead projector or for slides, simply leave the next step out.

2. Making the Ink Opaque With a *clean* ink roller apply white ink, starting above the previous layer of color. This makes the ink completely opaque and means that if, for example, you transfer lettering or symbols on to a background of a different color, the background will not show through. Now dry this layer of white with a hair dryer.

3. Applying the Adhesive Apply a layer of adhesive with the *adhesive* roller so that the transfer elements will stick when they are applied later. Once again, start somewhat above the last layer, and this time be sure that the adhesive coating covers the *entire* sheet. If any portion of the sheet is left uncovered by adhesive, the transfer elements will not stick to it when they are rubbed down later. Dry this coating immediately, too.

4. Applying the Photo Coat Starting above the last layer, apply the ultraviolet-sensitive photo coating (called Photo Coat) with the *photo* roller. This coating comes in 2 components and has to be mixed before application. The mixture can be kept for about a month if it is stored in a dark place in an airtight plastic

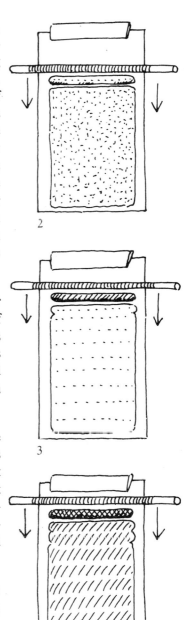

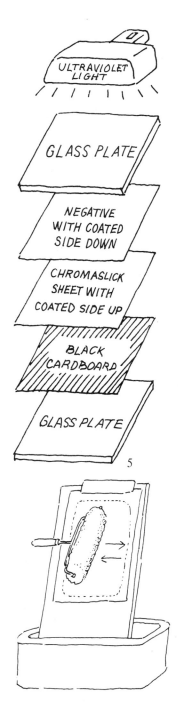

squeeze bottle that is impermeable to light. This layer, too, must be well dried.

5. Exposure   As an original, you need a film negative which, with its coated or emulsion side *up*, yields a right-reading image. Since your light source comes from above, this negative will have to be turned over so that the coated side faces *down* and you see a mirror image (wrong reading). Underneath the negative is the coated Chromaslick sheet with it coating *up*. If you do not have an exposure unit, then the order of the elements, starting from the top, is as follows:

> glass plate
> negative with coated side down
> Chromaslick sheet with coated side up
> black cardboard
> glass plate

Use an ultraviolet light source. Because lamps vary in intensity, you will have to test for the proper exposure time.

6. Rinsing with Water   Those portions of the photosensitive surface that the black areas of the negative have prevented from hardening are now rinsed away with a mohair roller dipped in clean water. Clamp the Chromatec sheet to a plate of glass with the coated side out. Set the glass at an angle, and pass the wet roller back and forth horizontally over the sheet until the coating dissolves. Rinse the last traces of the layer away with clean water and *carefully* dry the coated side of the sheet with a paper towel. Use a hair dryer to dry the sheet completely.

7. Developing   The developer is a chemical that dissolves the adhesive and the ink on the *unhardened* portions of the sheet. Clamp the Chromaslick sheet to the working surface, again with the coated side up. Now soak both sides of the foam-rubber developer pad in the developer and draw the pad lightly over the sheet 2 or 3 times. Let the developer work for 20 to 30 seconds. Because developing is a process of dissolving and not of rubbing, you have to exercise extreme caution here to avoid damaging the surface. Use the clean side of the developer pad now to remove the remaining ink and adhesive, and dry the sheet with the hair dryer.

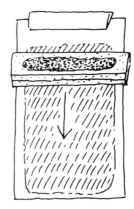

8. Removing the Photo Coat   There is still a photo-sensitive coating left on the *hardened* areas. This coating can now be removed with a Photo Coat solvent. Soak the bottom half of a cotton pad with the solvent and pass the pad lightly over the sheet, *without rubbing*, until this grayish layer is gone. As soon as the sheet is dry, the Chromatec transfer material can be rubbed off.

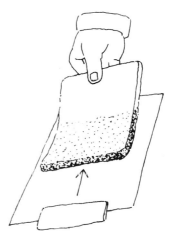

Once you are familiar with the process, it will take you about 10 to 20 minutes to prepare a Chromatec sheet, assuming that you are using a standard ink or a color mixture that is already prepared. You have to allow extra time to mix a color. Colors are mixed according to the instructions in the color mixing book. The adhesive is not present on the entire sheet but only on the portions that will eventually be transferred. This is particularly helpful if the transfer elements are to be rubbed off onto a film or a dark background.

Because the costs for setting up a work place and acquiring the necessary implements and materials are appreciable and because considerable practice is needed before you can work efficiently with the Chromatec process, it is cheaper and easier for someone who has only an occasional need for this medium to have Chromatec transfer materials prepared for him in a type shop.

Alkyd Paints

The firm of Winsor & Newton offers alkyd paints under the brand name Griffin and the more expensive brand, Artists' Alkyd. These paints behave like oil paints, can be mixed with oil mediums, but have an alkyd-resin base. Unlike normal oil paints, alkyd paints have the great advantage that they dry overnight, which makes them an ideal medium for illustration. Acrylic paints dry even faster, but with alkyd paints it is easier to produce soft transitions. Furthermore, the individual colors are richer and more transparent; it seems to me, too, that alkyd paints can be used much more sparingly.

Surfaces

Bristol board 3.4

Primer 2.18

As in oil painting, various surfaces or base materials can be used: paper, board, wood or masonite board, or canvas. For illustrations a 2-ply, smooth-surfaced Bristol Board (mounted on plywood with masking tape) is ideal. The paint does not soak through, and the work can be stretched afterwards on a scanner (which produces the screening for 4-color separation). Unprimed canvas, wood, or masonite can be primed with Gesso.

Application

There are 34 color tones, all of which dry equally quickly. They can be applied with oil brushes, with stippling brushes, or pieces of foam rubber. You can use paper towels to wipe or daub them into templates. Because they take longer to dry than acrylics, you can rub or smear them about for quite a while.

268

A retouching brush is excellent for doing fine details. With a paint mixed with Win-Gel and a brush tip with some paint thinner or rectified turpentine in it, you can produce fine lines.

Retouching brush 6.2

For work in normal formats the 20-mL tubes are altogether adequate. You should, however, buy larger tubes of Titan White, which is used for lightening. The price for all the colors is the same.

Mediums

Alkyd paints can be mixed with the usual oil mediums. However, there are 3 mediums that have been developed with an alkyd base and that share the advantage of relatively rapid drying time.

1. Liquin improves the malleability and flow of the paint, thereby making very fine tinting and details possible.
2. Win-Gel is a jellylike medium. As with Liquin, use a spatula to mix it with paint on your palette. (The more Win-Gel added, the more transparent the color will become.) With it, too, you can produce fine variations in tone. It does leave the brush structure visible, but you can remedy this by smoothing the area with a dry brush.

    Spatula 6.7
    Palette 6.6
3. Oleopasto is used to produce plastic brush strokes and for spatula work.

Special paper palettes are very handy for working with these paints.

Glazing

Because of their high transparency and brilliance, these paints are ideally suited for glazing. Mix the paint with either Liquin or Win-Gel and apply the first layer with brush, sponge, tissue, or whatever texturing material you intend to use. Another medium for this is rectified turpentine, which dries faster than the others. If you use certain paint thinners instead of rectified turpentine, the paint may crack after a certain time.

In comparison with acrylic paint, with alkyd paint you have a reasonable amount of time to work on transitions and to make corrections. The drying time depends on the amount of medium you use. Allow the surface to dry for 8 to 10 hours (overnight); though absolutely dry after this time, you can still dissolve the layer with turpentine or paint thinner.

In summertime you can expose the wet surface to direct sunlight (this may warp the Bristol board, but once out of the sun it flattens out again) to enhance the drying process, which can cut the drying time to 3 to 4 hours. In wintertime, however, placing the board face toward a radiator may help the drying time a bit.

With each layer, you can apply the color to create an enormous deepness, similar to a watercolor wash. This technique is ideal, especially for texturing effects. If you make a mistake in color or form, say during the second layer, simply wipe off the color with a paper tissue. If it does not come off entirely, use a soft paper tissue with a bit of turpentine or paint thinner, then remove the rest of it gingerly. After 6 to 9 months, it is useful to cover the piece of art with a final varnish. Clean the brushes with paint thinner, and afterwards, wash them with soap and water to keep them smooth.

Illustration for the Short Story series in *Zeit* magazine. Alkyd paints on cold-press, 2-ply, smooth mechanical board. The comp format was twice as large as the final printed format.

Practical Tips

Transfer Lettering

Transfer lettering 5.3

Copyproof materials 8.3

You can keep your costs down in working with transfer lettering like Letraset or Chartpac if you have access to a reprocamera and work with Copyproof or PMT. Instead of buying several sheets of the same type style in different sizes, buy only a 36-point sheet of 1 style. There are enough upper and lower case letters on such a sheet, and the size of the letters is suitable for relatively extreme enlargements and reductions. Transfer the words or lines you want; then use the reprocamera to convert them to the size you want.

Storing Mixed Acrylic Paints

If you are working with acrylics and are using a *mixed* paint for the background or a large area, it is always wise to mix a little more of the paint than you need for the first application. Put the remaining paint on a piece of aluminum foil and fold it into the foil so that as little air as possible is wrapped in with it. The paint can be kept for a few days this way should you have to retouch or make changes in the course of your work, which, with acrylics, may well extend over a few days. This extra packet of mixed paint may spare you the often very difficult task of matching your original color with a new mix.

Mixed acrylic paint can also be stored in empty film containers. To keep the air away from the paint, carefully pour a little water on top of it. When you want to use the paint, pour the water off (see also page 160).

Stippling with Acrylic Paint

After a first application of stippled acrylic paint is dry, use Scotch tape to lift off the paint remaining on the template. It may even be necessary to cut *lightly* around the edge of the form again with your template knife because the Scotch tape can sometimes take some of the paint inside the form, too. Because acrylic paint has the tendency to form a rubbery layer that does not stick firmly to the smooth acetate, the wet paint of your second application will loosen it, and lumps of it will cling to your brush or piece of foam rubber (see illustration, page 154, upper right).

Transferring a Drawing onto Frisk Film

There is a very efficient way to transfer a linear contour drawing onto frisk film for stippling or spraying.

Execute your drawing with a pencil that is not too hard (for example, a 2B) on a plate-finished drawing paper 2, 3, or 4-ply or, better yet, on a thin illustration board. You can also use a heavy vellum paper. Lay the frisk film with its adhesive side down on the drawing. The adhesive will pick up some of the graphite, and when you carefully lift the acetate off again, you will have the entire drawing permanently fixed to the back side of the acetate. Now all you need to do is attach the frisk film to your background or base. Make a test first to be sure the surface of your paper doesn't stick to your adhesive frisk film.

Frisket 5.4

Storing Composite Tracings

It often happens that even work that has been accepted may need to be changed or reworked at a later date. For this reason it is always a good idea to keep your composite tracings, which are usually done on thin tracing paper. The rolls that tracing paper come on are ideal for storing these drawings. A roll of about 14″ x 50 yards is adequate for most drawings.

Tracing paper 3.2

273

With work incorporating color, it can also be useful to note the numbers or names of the paints or inks used, possibly even details of the mixed colors, too, and to store these notes with the records of the project or job.

Making Screens

Screens 5.2

For the screen procedures described on pages 228 and following, you can use commercially available screens (most of which have adhesive on the back) to make your own screens. Using the Copyproof system, you can make enlargements, reductions, and, of course, 1:1 duplications of screens on CPF (transparent acetate). Screens or structures created manually or photographically, once put on film, can also be used for screen work.

Dr. Martin's Watercolors

Liquid aniline watercolors 2.19

These liquid watercolors can be used like tempera if you mix them with Dr. Martin's Flo-White. The results are paints that cover well and produce very delicate pastel tones.

If you add Dr. Martin's Flex-opaque to this mixture in 2:1 proportion, you get an acetate paint that covers well on film and smooth surfaces and that will neither crack nor peel.

Color Works as Originals for Printing

Scanners are being used more and more these days to produce color separations for printing. The original is stretched over a drum and then scanned electronically or with a laser scanner. I used to do a lot of my work on a thick illustration board, but it could happen that if the grain of this board were not lined up parallel with the drum the originals would come back with cracks in them. Some graphic artists combat this problem by splitting the board, but that is a risky business. The better solution is to use something like a 2-ply plate-finished board, which can be stretched on the drum easily and without risk of damage.

Bristol board 3.4

Perspective Grids

If you have to work with perspective, which a graphic designer is often required to do, there are now grids with a large range of perspectives printed on them. The blue lines used for these perspectives do not appear in photo reproductions, but they are heavy enough to be visible through tracing or layout paper. You can therefore either work directly on the grid or on a transparent material laid over it.

Copyproof Material That Will Take Color

There is a new, matte positive material (CPPm), which, after rinsing, should be squeegeed with the *coated side down* because the emulsion is not as firmly bonded to the carrier material as it is on CPP.

The matte surface can be colored with soft colored pencils, chalk, watercolors, felt-tipped markers, and so on.

Hints for Making Type Layouts

Lines of type or parts of a mobile layout that you will have to move often until you have found the proper place for them should be sprayed *very lightly* with a spray adhesive. This light coating of adhesive will make them stick firmly enough so that they will not slide around, yet it will also allow you to peel them off again easily and reposition them.

The positive paper CPPab and the positive film CPFab in the Copyproof line both have adhesive backing, which is a great help in producing montages that include lettering or pictorial elements.

Trim Sizes

Books, brochures, folders, and magazines will often fall outside common sizes because, on the one hand, their size is dictated by paper-making formats and, on the other, not every graphic artist likes these normed formats and so will create his or her own printing formats.

Watercolor pads or sheets as well as mechanical and Bristol board come in all kinds of sizes.

If you want to print something using an unusual format, it is a good idea to discuss the project with your printer before you even begin your planning and drafting. An unusual format may require the printer to use far more paper than one would expect, or it may be either uneconomical or impossible to handle on the machinery he has.

Cropping
The crop is, in the exact sense of the word, the edge of a printed object that is cut away when the bookbinder does his final trimming of the object. It is also often referred to as the trim.

Let's assume that you want to prepare a mechanical for printing in an 8½" x 11 (DIN A 2) format in which your subject will bleed and be trimmed on all 4 sides after printing. To ensure that you will have sufficient margin around your 8½" x 11" (DIN A 2) format, use a painting or sketching board that is approximately 12½" x 15" (500 x 700 mm). That will give you about 2" (53 mm) to spare on all sides.

Measure in 2" (40 mm) from the left-hand edge of the board and, using a sharp hard pencil (4-9H) and a long ruler or T-square, make 2 small crop mark lines about ½" to ¾" (1 to 2 cm) long on the top and bottom of the page. From these lines, measure 8½" (420 mm) to the right, and set 2 more small lines. Now measure 2" (53 mm) down from the upper left- and right-hand corners, and make your lines. From these, measure down 11" (594 mm) to establish your lower crop line. Go over these 8 crop marks with a fine technical pen (0.13 - 0.25).

Measure out ¼" (5 mm) from these marks all the way around, and draw a thin pencil line around what is now your working format of 9" x 11½" (430 x 604 mm); that is, 8½" + 2 x ¼", = 9"; 11" + 2 x ¼" bleed − 11½" (420 mm ╵ 2 x 5 mm bleed = 430 mm; 594 + 2 x 5 mm bleed = 604 mm).

As a rule ³/₁₆" (3 mm) is enough to allow, but for safety's sake I allow between ¼" and ³/₈" (5 and 10 mm) crop for large-format work.

You can run Scotch tape or masking tape around your thin pencil line to ensure a clean edge later. Always draw the outlines of your final cropped area on an overlay of tracing paper or acetate.

It is extremely important to allow enough margin not only for printed objects but also for originals that will be filmed (animations or TV films) or photographically reproduced (slides for projections of any kind). In this latter case, the terms normally used are "margin" or safety margin, not "crop." Depending on the size of the original, this margin can amount to an inch or so (a few cm) on each side. The view-finders on cameras are not always as precise as one would wish.

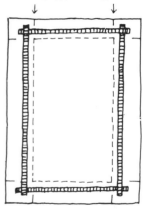

CROP LINES

Presentation of Comps

For presenting comps (comprehensives), layouts, and artwork to customers you can mount your work on white, gray, or black illustration board. You can use either rubber cement or a spray adhesive, the latter being available in both a permanent and a removable

Exhibit board 3.6

Rubber cement 7.1

277

type. Work mounted this way has the advantage of always looking smooth and orderly.

I often prefer the foam board (Fome-Cor) material to white illustration board, which weighs more and is more difficult to cut. Foam board material is bulkier (a thickness of ca. $^3/_{16}''$ (5 mm) is adequate for most purposes), but it can be easily cut with a sharp utility knife and cutting ruler.

Utility knife 6.8
Cutting straight edge 1.24

Mounting without a Margin (Flush Mounting)

A mounting without a margin is sometimes the preferred form for originals such as sketches, layouts, and similar items that are intended specifically for presentations or for copies or prints made from originals. In this form, the mounting board is exactly the same size as the artwork itself, and there are several ways you can prepare such a mounting.

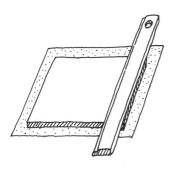

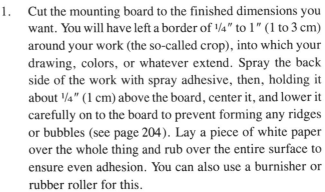

1. Cut the mounting board to the finished dimensions you want. You will have left a border of $^1/_4''$ to 1 $''$ (1 to 3 cm) around your work (the so-called crop), into which your drawing, colors, or whatever extend. Spray the back side of the work with spray adhesive, then, holding it about $^1/_4''$ (1 cm) above the board, center it, and lower it carefully on to the board to prevent forming any ridges or bubbles (see page 204). Lay a piece of white paper over the whole thing and rub over the entire surface to ensure even adhesion. You can also use a burnisher or rubber roller for this.

   If you are using foam board, be *very careful* in this operation because the foam material is easily damaged by pressure. Now turn board and work over, and use a utility knife and cutting ruler to cut off the overhanging edge of the work.

2. Spray the work with adhesive, and lay it on your worktable with the adhesive side up. Center the board over the work, and proceed as described above.

3. Cut both the work and the mounting board larger than the finished format. Glue them together, mark the first finished edge (with 2 light, short marks on the left and right-hand sides outside the finished format), and then cut the edge off with your knife and ruler. Now lay a large right-angle triangle on that finished edge, mark the second finished edge, cut it off, and proceed in the same fashion with the remaining sides.

If you have used white illustration board, it is easier to make only the first cut with knife and ruler and to use a paper cutter (which, of course, should cut at an exact right angle) to cut the remaining 3 sides. A paper cutter will not, however, make a clean cut with foam board because the foam crumbles on the cut edges. A knife is the ideal tool for this material.

Mounting with a Margin (Mat)

Cut the backing board the same size as your mat will be. Now draw the picture format on the back of the mat board, and cut it out. Tape the inside of the mat to the upper edge of the backing board so that you can slide your work in from below. Position the work where you want it within the cutout, hold it down firmly, and mark its corners on the backing board.

Now, using tape, rubber cement, or spray adhesive, you can glue down the work, which should be *larger* than the cutout area in the mat. Or, if you are mounting originals you will be working with again after the presentation, fasten them to the backing board with masking tape. Now close or mount the mat over the work (see also section on mats).

The Portfolio

The format of the portfolio that a graphic artist who has just graduated from school will have often depends on the formats his or her teachers required. Some teachers swear by huge formats; others, by miniatures that seem no larger than postage stamps.

You should try as best you can to impose some order and unity on your portfolio and not be required to fish out both framed and unframed work of every possible size when you are making a presentation. Bristol and illustration boards (15" x 20" [50 x 65 cm]) are preferred and fit available portfolio cases. These boards have proved adequate, economical, and handy in size. If necessary, the work under the mats is protected with acetate or removable tracing or layout paper. The mats should be cleanly cut with a sharp knife. Bristol board comes in different thicknesses, so choose the thickness that the work you will use under it requires. If the work has waves in it, use a heavier board. As a rule, however, relatively thin board suffices. The work should not be placed arbitrarily in space. Place it slightly above the optic center. I personally think it is better to cut a few extra mats so that you can show each piece of work *individually*, even with works in tiny formats; and I do not care for colored mats. White, gray, or black are altogether adequate. Seek advice from your teachers on which work and how much you will put in your portfolio (assuming that you value their advice). Advice is free, and it is often the case that an outsider can judge your work better than you can yourself.

Some agency art directors swear by ring binders with transparent pockets. For an artist already well along in his profession, that is a very practical arrangement because he will be able to show enough printed work that fits somewhere between these two formats. But a new graduate, who will not have worked exclusively in these formats during his entire course of study, would have either to enlarge or reduce his work to fit them.

For black-and-white work, you can make reductions either with Copyproof or—much cheaper—with a photostat machine that can either enlarge or reduce. For color work this can run into money. Good color prints are very expensive, and with Copycolor or Ciba-chrome, you have to expect color reproduction somewhat below the mark. It's questionable whether the expense is worth it.

You should always present your portfolio in person. It is obvious that you can best represent and explain yourself and your work in a personal meeting. I strongly advise against sending your portfolio anywhere. First, you should *never* let your originals out of your sight; second, you can't know when and in what condition you will get your portfolio back.

You can, of course, make slides of your work and send them out in slotted acetate holders. One very practical holder is the common slide sheet which holds 20 35 mm slides. It is flat, and the user can hold it up to the light to look at the slides.

I have had good luck with color slide indoor film, but let me give you a tip. If you are going to go to the trouble of photographing your work, selecting certain sections, taking off acetate or other protective covers to avoid glare, and so on, then you should make several slides of the same item. It is simpler and cheaper to snap the shutter 5 or 6 times than it is to go through the whole process again or have duplicates made. In this way, you can send out several sets of pictures at once without having to wait for the return of your one and only set.

Illustration by Georges Lacroix from the magazine *La Maison de Marie-Claire*. This illustration was used in an article on haunted houses called "Houses That Kill." Art Director, Daniel Lattes. Acrylic on board. The entire picture was executed in tones of gray, which emphasize the threatening nature of the subject.

Glossary

This glossary contains only terms that are referred to directly in this book. Secondary meanings are not included, because they would unnecessarily complicate the information conveyed here.

Airbrush
A pistol-like device that uses compressed air or carbon dioxide to spray paint.

Blending
Drawing technique done with pencil or colored pencil to create soft transitions.

Blending Stumps
Round sticks of gray paper, pointed at one or both ends. By rubbing with a blending stump, you can create fields and progressions of shading in pencil, colored pencil, and pastels.

Centering Tack
A thumbtacklike device with a small depression in the middle that acts as the stationary leg of a compass. It is used whenever repeated use of a compass might widen the center hole in a circle and so make it impossible to draw precise circles.

Collage
A composition made up of different materials (usually paper, printing, photographs) that are pasted together on a surface, often one over another.

Color Separation
Manual or photomechanical separation of a halftone original into films of gray or individual colors. Photomechanical color separation is done by making exposures of varying lengths on high-contrast, line-conversion materials.

Coloring (Tinting)
Hand coloring of drawings or photographs, usually done with watercolors.

Copy
A reproduction made from an original with a copy machine on a scale of 1:1 or larger or smaller.

Copy-Board Original/Back-Lit Original
The first term describes an original that is *not* transparent. The second term, by contrast, describes an original that *is* transparent; it is usually a transparency, a piece of film, or an original in some other transparent material. It is lit from below or behind.

Crop
That part of the margin of any printed matter—whether book, poster, brochure, or whatever—that is cut away when the bookbinder trims the finished product. As a rule, the crop amounts to between $1/2''$ and $2''$ on each trimmed side.

Cutting Blade
A scalpel-shaped knife insert used in a compass to cut out circles.

Decalcomania
Ink or color is spread on a plate of glass. The surface that will take the picture is then laid on this layer of ink or color and pressed down. Textured fields of color are transferred in a soft quality.

Dummy
A 3-dimensional model; also, a book with empty pages that shows the size and thickness the actual finished book will have. Dummy and mock-up are used more or less interchangeably.

Dummy Copy
Randomly selected text that is mounted in a layout to show the style and size of type, with the appropriate line spacing and overall dimensions with which the actual text will be printed.

Felt-Tipped Markers/Visualizing Paper
Marker colors show up in full brilliance on this special semitransparent paper through which images with strong contrasts can be seen. Colors will not bleed through on a good visualizing paper.

Fixing

Spray a fixative onto a pencil, charcoal, or pastel drawing to prevent smudging.

4-Color Process

The printing of the 4 primary printing inks—yellow, magenta (red), cyan (blue), and black—over each other to reproduce full-color images.

Graphite

A carbon used in pencils and graphite paper.

Gray Scale

A strip of photographic paper or film that is divided into fields ranging from white through increasingly dark shades of gray and ending with black. These gray scales can have as many as 20 gradations. They are used to determine the precise exposure times needed for repro material, ColorKey, Chromatec, and so on. When the gray scale is exposed along with a test exposure, certain shades of gray need to appear if the proper exposure has been used.

Gray Value

The degree of blackness of a given gray in a halftone picture or the equivalent gray value of a color.

Grids and Screens

1. A grid consists of a network of evenly spaced vertical and horizontal lines or modules. Magazine layouts are always based on specially designed grids that aid in establishing the size of the lettering and of the columns as well as the placement of text and pictures.

2. Screens are available in a multitude of forms for photographic and overlay purposes. They can be classified by the type, number, arrangement, and mixture of grid elements. The most common patterns are line screens (parallel lines), cross-section graph screens (vertical and horizontal lines crossing each other), dot screens (network of regularly distributed dots), mezzotint screens (dots of varying size and in irregular placement), progression screens (network of elements that become stronger or weaker in density or that are separated from each other in intervals that increase or decrease in size at a steady rate; depending on the fineness of the elements and the distance from which they are viewed, they can simulate progression in a color).

Halftone

A black-and-white photograph so called because it contains all the tones of gray that lie between full black and white. What's essential is that the transitions between the grays are *fluid*. Halftone material can be bought as paper or film.

High-Contrast Photograph

A photographic copy on paper or film that shows only pure black and pure white. The print has no gray values; and hence the original is reduced to lines, dots, and solid fields. Only high-contrast films and papers will yield this kind of result.

Highlights

Light areas, reflections, or shiny areas on figures or objects.

Impasto Paint

Unthinned paint applied just as it comes out of the jar or tube.

Layout

1. A complete design mock-up in black and white or in color that may include dummy copy or an actual text to simulate the final printed work. Layouts are used primarily for making presentations to clients, but if they are equipped with instructions, they can also serve as detailed guides for a photographer, an artist executing the finished work, a typesetter, a repro photographer, or a printer.

2. The term *layout* has also taken on the extended meaning of the organization of pictures and text in a book, magazine, or ad.

Line Drawing

This technical concept in printing means that all the strokes, lines, dots, and color fields in a picture are done normally in *pure* black and can be photographed on high-contrast materials. In terms of this definition, a line drawing done in pencil (because it is not *pure* black) is a halftone original.

Lucy (Lucigraph)

An optical drawing machine used for enlargement or reduction of drawings.

Mat

Removable paper or cardboard frame that is laid over a picture or photograph to:

1. Cover unimportant parts.
2. Show only a certain portion.
3. Protect the work.
4. Provide a frame of whatever dimensions the artist chooses for the work.

Mechanical

Final stage of a design when it is ready to serve as an original for photomechanical reproduction. It may be a layout or a finished picture in one piece, or it may consist of several overlays lined up together with the aid of register marks.

Medium

Material in which a work is executed, such as acrylic paint or watercolors, as well as additives to paints and inks.

Mixed Techniques

Painting procedure in which a picture is created by combining 2 or more techniques with different media or different techniques with the same media.

Mobile Layout

Composing technique in which individual elements are cut out so they can be moved around until a final layout is agreed upon. When the composition has reached the desired state, the parts will be tacked down with Scotch tape or glued down (on spots only) with rubber cement.

Mock-Up

A model or other representation on a 1:1 scale; for example, a simulated package, book, or ad.

Moiré

An optical effect produced by the misalignment of 2 or more dense screens.

Montage

Pasting individual elements, such as photographs, lettering, text, on board or film on film. This is usually done with rubber cement or adhesives.

One-to-One (1:1)

The scale in which a copy or drawing or photograph is the same size as the original.

Opaque

Used to describe paints that cover thoroughly; opposite of transparent.

Original

Any kind of artwork that is used as a basis for further reproduction.

Out-of-Register Printing

The blank space that shows if 2 neighboring fields of color do not meet exactly and that lets the paper show through.

Overlay

A transparent or translucent sheet of acetate, layout paper, or tracing paper that is ordinarily fastened over an original with tape. It is used to draw on, to color on, to make notes on, to cover over, to make changes in certain areas of a work, or to separate artwork in different colors from that of the base mechanical.

Palette

Usually an oval or rectangular plate made of wood, glass, or metal with or without indentations in it; used for holding and mixing paints.

Photostat

A copy made in a stat camera on photosensitive paper in a negative or direct positive.

Pigment
Particulate coloring matter used in suspension.

Polymer Medium
A colorless medium used in acrylic paints.

Processors
Machines used for developing photosensitive material. Negative and positive papers pass through a developing bath and are squeezed together and moved forward by rollers.

Progression
A flowing, uninterrupted transition between light and dark or between 2 or more colors.

Register Marks
Small and very thin crosses measuring about $\frac{1}{2}''$ (1 cm) that are put on an original and on any overlays to make it possible to replace the overlays in the correct position if they are removed or if they slip. They are also used by printers to achieve perfect registration.

Rendering
Full-color representation of space, landscape, and objects, done by hand usually.

Repro (abbreviation for Reproduction)
High-quality copy on paper or film made with a stat camera; most often refers to the type to be pasted up. A repro is better than a normal copy.

Retarder
Slows down the drying process in acrylics and makes it easier to paint shadings.

Screening
Breaking down a halftone original into individual elements like dots, lines, or grain. Each of these elements, no matter how small, is made up of a solid area.

Scribble
Like a thumbnail sketch, this is a first, rapidly executed, and very rough sketch that records ideas, information, sequences of events, figures, or objects and provides a preliminary sketch for presentation and discussion.

Shading/Crosshatching
Created in drawings by mechanically or manually executed lines usually arranged parallel to each other. That done with lines that cross each other is called *crosshatching*.

Solid Color
Deepest intensity (100%) of a color on a surface; an unscreened color.

Stabilizer
An image-producing liquid used in copying machines that acts as a developer *and* a fixative.

Stippling
Application of impasto paint with a special or specially equipped brush; almost always done with the aid of templates.

Template
A guide used to draw or paint a precise shape. The object to be depicted is cut out of the template material (paper, cardboard, acetate), leaving a negative form. After stippling or spraying, paint is only on the area left open in the template.

Varnish Brush
A wide brush used to apply a finishing varnish to a completed picture. The lacquer produces a uniform surface (glossy or matte) and protects the picture from dirt and injury. This brush can also be used to build up large fields of color.

Wash
Application of a highly diluted paint that lets the ground and any other previously applied colors show through.

Work Drawing/Tracing
A drawing made on tracing paper and often transferred to another working surface.

Index

287

288